TWICE AHEAD

How to Build an Agent-Powered Business Before
Your Industry Catches Up

Thomas Heimann

Twice Ahead Publishing

Published by Twice Ahead Publishing, Land O' Lakes, Florida

ISBN (Paperback): 979-8-9955444-1-8
ISBN (Ebook): 979-8-9955444-0-1
Library of Congress Control Number: 2026908732

www.ThomasHeimann.com

For Jennifer. Everything I build, I build with you.

Contents

Introduction

I've seen this movie before.

I don't say that as a line. I say it because I was there the last time a technology wave this big started separating the people who would build the future from the people who would spend the next decade reacting to it.

In 1994, most business owners had no idea what was coming. Compuserve had just introduced WinCIM. Prodigy and AOL were still in their early stages. The commercial internet was not yet understood by the average entrepreneur, and the few people paying attention often misunderstood it badly. The Canter & Siegel green card lottery scandal had just put online marketing on the map for all the wrong reasons. A lot of people saw the internet as a place to blast messages, game the system, and grab attention by any means necessary.

I saw something else.

I saw a new communications infrastructure. Direct access. Speed. Leverage. A moment when small entrepreneurs could suddenly compete in ways that had never been possible before.

That distinction mattered then, and it matters now.

Back then, I began teaching entrepreneurs how to use online services and the internet properly. Not as spammers. Not as opportunists chasing gimmicks. Strategically. Ethically. I created a course called Computer Profits, and later the All In One Electronic Marketing Kit. Those weren't academic products. They were built for people who wanted to generate business in a new environment but didn't yet understand the rules.

Email was quickly becoming the primary marketing tool inside that world, and

I ran into the same problem every serious operator ran into at scale: responding manually didn't work. The opportunity was real, but the workflow was broken.

So I built the first autoresponder.

That word is common now. In 1994, it wasn't. I coined the term because I needed language for something that didn't yet have a category. That happened more than once in those years. When you reach a frontier early enough, you find yourself naming things before the market understands why they matter.

That's one of the clearest signals you're standing at the edge of a real shift.

* * *

Most people, even smart people, assume the early stage of a new technology is the technology. It isn't. It's the crude first expression of it.

In the early internet era, people thought online services were the story. They thought email was the story. Bulletin boards and chat rooms were the story. They were looking at the visible surface and assuming they were seeing the whole machine.

What they were seeing was the doorway.

By late 1994, it became obvious to me that the World Wide Web would be the future for business. Not in some vague sense. Not as a hobby. As the infrastructure layer beneath everything that came next.

That realization changed everything.

Once I saw it clearly, I stopped thinking like a marketer using online tools and started thinking like a builder of infrastructure. If businesses were going to move onto the web, they would need domains. They would need hosting. They would need email. They would need a way to establish a real presence—not just rent attention inside someone else's system.

So I built what became the world's first real web hosting company, with online domain registration, free of charge, and hosted email. That sounds normal now. In 1995, it wasn't normal at all.

We first called it the Global Entrepreneurs Network. Later, we shortened it to GEN.

GEN was not built from the perspective of a giant enterprise. It was built from the perspective I understood best: the entrepreneur trying to move faster than the market, with fewer resources than the incumbents, but with more urgency and better instincts.

That became a recurring pattern in my life.

* * *

I've always been drawn to moments when a structural advantage becomes available to outsiders before insiders realize the rules have changed.

That pattern didn't start with the internet.

I was born in Germany in 1965. My childhood was unstable, and I learned early that if I wanted a different future, I'd have to build it myself. I was fascinated by computers long before I could afford one. I spent time in department stores working on demo machines, writing BASIC programs from memory, learning by experimentation because there was no other option. I came to the United States at twenty-one with about two hundred dollars and limited English.

When you start that way, you don't become theoretical about opportunity. You get practical very fast.

My early businesses in the United States were not glamorous. Mobile auto detailing. Newspaper fundraising ads. A telemarketing-driven carpet cleaning business. They taught me direct response, sales, speed, and the brutal clarity of market feedback. You learn quickly when you're spending money you can't afford to waste.

You also learn that small entrepreneurs don't need more inspiration nearly as much as they need more leverage.

That belief shaped everything I did in the internet era, and it shapes everything I believe about AI now.

GEN grew into the largest web hosting company in the world—more than 35,000 domains, over 10,000 customers, reach into more than 30 countries. Along the way, I built the first web-based domain registration service. We developed the first true Microsoft IIS hosting farm and the first Microsoft FrontPage hosting provider. We created what was, in effect, the first real combination of ecommerce and hosting in one integrated environment. We partnered on initiatives like the eBusiness CD-ROM with Microsoft and AOL because I believed then, as I do now, that when a wave this large is forming, the smart move is not to admire it. The smart move is to build on it.

That period gave me something more valuable than revenue.

It gave me pattern recognition.

I got to watch, in real time, what happens when the market misreads a shift of that magnitude. First, most people dismiss it. Then some play with it in shallow ways. Then a few builders recognize that the real value isn't in using the new thing occasionally—it's in redesigning systems around it. Then the market wakes up and acts as though the outcome was obvious all along.

It never is. It only looks obvious in retrospect.

* * *

That is exactly where we are with AI agents right now.

A lot of people are still treating AI as a toy, a novelty, or at best a productivity assistant. They use it to clean up an email, summarize a document, generate a social media caption. I use those capabilities too. There's nothing wrong with that.

But if that's your full understanding of what's happening, you're looking at AI the way people looked at email in 1994.

You're seeing the surface, not the system.

The real opportunity is not AI as a clever tool. It's AI as architecture. As workflow. As an operating layer. It's AI in the form of agents that can monitor, route, research, draft, escalate, remember, coordinate, and execute within defined boundaries—under human oversight.

That is a completely different category from asking ChatGPT to write you a nicer paragraph.

And once you understand that distinction, you can't unsee it.

* * *

This is why I wrote this book.

Not because AI is interesting. Not because there's hype around it and everyone wants an opinion. I wrote it because I believe the next generation of business winners is being decided right now, and most entrepreneurs still don't understand what game they're actually in.

This is not a book about prompts or shiny tools. It's not for people who want to feel current without changing anything structural.

It's a book about what happens when a founder recognizes a technology shift early enough to redesign the company before the market catches up.

I've done that before. I'm doing it again now.

Today, one of my core operating companies is Cloud Title, a Florida title and settlement company. That's not a Silicon Valley software startup. It's a real operating business in a regulated, detail-heavy industry that still runs on a surprising amount of friction, repetition, fragmentation, and manual labor. In other words, it's exactly the kind of environment where intelligent workflows, agentic systems, and human-led AI deployment can create real advantage.

And I want to be clear: this transformation is not finished. We're not pretending to have solved everything. Cloud Title is in the early stages of its AI buildout. We use Qualia as our core production platform. We've adopted Qualia Clear. We're building automations around the business—an automated transaction coordinator, lien search systems, assistant functions, and frameworks to connect operating data to marketing and follow-up. We're learning in real time what works, what breaks, where governance matters, and where human oversight has to stay strong.

That honesty matters to me. I have no interest in writing a book that makes everything sound cleaner or more complete than it really is. I'm not interested in polished fantasy. I'm interested in practical truth.

At the same time, I'm building OpenClaw—a multi-agent AI operating environment running on my own infrastructure, with specialized agents handling research, content, engineering, operations, strategy, and other functions. That system is early. It's evolving. It's messy in places and powerful in others, and full of lessons about what an agent-powered business looks like when you stop thinking in terms of isolated tools and start thinking in terms of coordinated digital labor.

That phrase—digital labor—matters. Because that's what most people still don't understand.

The companies that win in the next decade won't simply be the ones that "use AI." That phrase is already too vague to mean much. The winners will be the ones that build human-led, agent-powered organizations. They'll know which work stays with people, which work gets delegated to systems, how trust should be calibrated, how memory and governance should be structured, and how to build a business where each intelligent layer compounds the others.

That's a much bigger conversation than software. It's a conversation about company design.

* * *

When I look back at 1994, what stands out most isn't the technology. It's how few people understood the second-order effects. They saw email but not direct response at scale. They saw websites but not digital distribution reshaping customer acquisition. They saw domain names but not digital real estate. They saw hosting but not the infrastructure layer beneath the next generation of commerce.

We're making the same mistake right now. People see content generation but not autonomous support functions. They see chatbots but not role-based digital workers. They see research assistance but not multi-agent execution environments. They see productivity hacks but not the redesign of the org chart.

And because they don't see those things clearly, they're moving too slowly.

The window is open right now. It won't stay open forever.

That's another lesson from the first time. In the beginning, the pioneer advantage feels almost unfair. There's room to move, room to experiment, room to look strange, room to make category-defining moves before the incumbents mobilize and the language hardens around the market. Then the window starts to close. More money enters. More noise. More consultants. More companies rush in with half-understood strategies. The real builders keep building, but the easy lead disappears.

If you want asymmetric advantage, you have to move while other people are still debating vocabulary.

* * *

That is what "twice ahead" means to me.

It means recognizing the shape of the future early enough to act before the consensus forms. It means refusing to confuse familiarity with understanding. It means knowing the crowd is usually late on structural change because they almost always evaluate the new through the lens of the old.

It means understanding that if you're only using a new technology to make your old model slightly more efficient, you may be missing the real opportunity entirely.

And it means having the courage to build while the picture is still incomplete.

That last part matters. Every genuine frontier looks messy in real time. The early internet was messy—the companies, the infrastructure, the customer education, the market. That didn't make the opportunity less real. It made it more real, because frontiers are messy precisely because they're being formed.

AI agents are in that stage now. Some of the tools are impressive. Some are overhyped. Some are genuinely useful. New categories will emerge. Old assumptions will break. Standards will form. Great businesses will be built. A lot of nonsense will be sold in the process.

None of that changes the core point.

The shift is real. The economic implications are real. And the founders who learn to build around it early will have a structural advantage that late adopters will struggle to close.

* * *

This book is my attempt to make that advantage visible.

Not from the perspective of a commentator on the sidelines. From the perspective of someone who has lived through one major technology revolution, built in it early, made real mistakes, built real companies, and now finds himself at the edge of another one that looks far more consequential than most people realize.

I'm not asking you to admire AI. I'm asking you to read the moment correctly.

If you're an entrepreneur, founder, executive, or business owner, this moment concerns you whether you feel ready or not. It concerns your margins, your speed, your customer experience, your staffing model, your decision cycles, your sales process, your scalability, and ultimately the value of the business you're building.

The question is not whether AI will matter.

The question is whether you'll use this period to redesign your company while the window is still open.

I've seen what happens when people miss a moment like this. I've also seen what happens when they catch it early.

That's what this book is about.

The first time, the internet changed how business was done. This time, agents will change how businesses are built.

The winners are being decided now.

Part I:
The Pattern

Chapter 1

The Internet Was Supposed to Be a Fax Machine

T he internet was not supposed to become what it became.

That sounds obvious now, which is exactly why it matters.

When people first heard about the internet in the early 1990s, they didn't imagine digital commerce, cloud infrastructure, SaaS, social networks, creator economies, or trillion-dollar companies built on a protocol stack most people couldn't explain. They thought in smaller, safer terms. They thought email was a fax machine.

That was the metaphor. Not a new economy. Not a new operating system for business. Just a better fax.

To be fair, that wasn't irrational. Fax machines were still fresh in business culture. Before that, many businesses relied on telex. Fax had already felt like a miracle—documents moved faster, deals moved faster, communication sped up. So when the internet entered the conversation, most people translated it through the last thing they understood.

Email equals fax. That was the box.

And once people put a new technology in the wrong box, they stay blind to its real implications for far too long.

I remember that era clearly because I was living inside it. I wasn't watching as a commentator. I was building in it.

The World Wide Web was slow, ugly, awkward, and expensive. That part gets forgotten. People look back as if the internet arrived fully formed, wearing a suit, carrying a business plan. It didn't. Early web pages were primitive. Connections were slow. The user experience was terrible.

Most people got online through AOL or CompuServe. You'd dial in through a modem, listen to the noise, wait for the handshake. Then, if everything worked, you could branch out. In many cases you needed a separate dialer to connect to an ISP. Once connected, you launched separate programs—Netscape for the web, Eudora for email. Nothing was intuitive. Nothing was seamless. It was not ready.

That mattered because immature technology always looks smaller than it really is. People judge the future by the current interface. That's one of the most expensive mistakes an entrepreneur can make.

If you looked at the early web and judged it only by what it was in that moment, you would have missed the whole thing. Too slow, too technical, too limited, too expensive, too niche. You would have had plenty of evidence to sound intelligent while being completely wrong.

That happens in every major shift. The first version is crude. The use cases are narrow. The public thinks in analogies borrowed from the past. Experts explain why it won't scale. Incumbents protect their assumptions. The new thing gets reduced to a toy, a side channel, or a threat associated with fringe behavior.

We saw it with the internet. We saw it with Bitcoin—reduced to "internet money for criminals" while almost nobody asked the more important question: what happens if the underlying architecture matters more than the current surface behavior?

We're seeing it again with AI agents.

The public doesn't usually miss the future because they're stupid. They miss it because the future arrives wrapped in an immature version of itself—before the interface is polished, before the infrastructure is stable, before the pricing makes sense, before the mainstream understands the point. And because of that, the people best positioned to see the shift often dismiss it first.

That includes experts. In fact, experts are often the last to see it.

That sounds backwards, but it isn't. Experts are trained by the current system. Their expertise is built on how things work now—the rules, the economics, the bottlenecks, the accepted best practices. Useful in stable environments. Dangerous during transitions. When a real shift shows up, they interpret it through the old framework, asking whether this new thing fits the existing category. The better question is whether the category itself is about to break.

In the early internet days, established business people asked whether the web would become a better brochure, a better catalog, a better communication tool. Those weren't crazy questions. They were just too small. The entrepreneurs who moved early weren't the ones who answered those questions best. They were the ones who asked a different question altogether: What if this becomes the default infrastructure for how business communicates, markets, sells, delivers, recruits, educates, and scales?

That turned out to be the right question.

I came into that moment with a specific lens. I wasn't looking at the internet as a corporate executive protecting a legacy system. I was looking at it as an entrepreneur who understood what it felt like to operate without the resources the big players had.

I saw the web as a great equalizer. That was the big idea for me.

A small business that got online affordably could look bigger than it was. It could reach outside its local geography, market without buying traditional media, communicate at scale, present itself with more authority. It could compete in ways previously reserved for companies with bigger budgets.

There was only one problem. Small businesses couldn't afford it.

That contradiction was the opportunity.

On paper, the web could level the playing field. In reality, early websites were expensive and difficult to build. Hosting was expensive. Domain registration was cumbersome. The very tool that should have opened the door for entrepreneurs was priced and packaged in a way that kept many of them out.

I saw that gap and decided to build around it.

That was the beginning of GEN, the Global Entrepreneurs Network.

The idea was straightforward: create a membership-based organization that made web hosting affordable for entrepreneurs and small business owners. We offered hosting starting at around $30 a month. That sounds ordinary now. At the time, it was a wedge—a way of saying this technology should not belong only to bigger companies or technical insiders.

Few people saw the full vision then. Even among people who wanted "a website," many thought of it as a novelty or a checkbox. A digital business card. They weren't yet thinking in terms of online customer acquisition, ecommerce, information products, backend automation, or platform effects. That maturity took years.

It took roughly a decade for the internet to mature into what most people now take for granted. That's another pattern people miss: when a platform shift begins, the early believers are directionally right long before the economics, tooling, and design catch up.

Being early rarely feels comfortable. The market usually makes you look wrong before it makes you look right.

That's where conviction matters. Not blind conviction. Pattern-based conviction.

Blind conviction says, "I feel this is going to be big." Pattern-based conviction says, "I've seen enough underlying signals to know this matters, even though the current version still looks rough."

The internet gave off those signals early. Even with all its friction, it was obvious to me the web would become the future. Not because the first websites were great—they weren't. Not because the user experience was polished—it wasn't. It was obvious because the architecture changed the economics.

That's the heart of it.

Whenever a technology changes the economics of access, distribution, communication, coordination, or production, pay attention. Not because every company in that wave will win—most won't. Not because the timing is easy—it isn't. But because once the economics shift, the old assumptions stop being safe.

The internet changed the economics of presence. Before the web, if you wanted reach, authority, or distribution at scale, you needed physical infrastructure, traditional media, a bigger sales footprint, or a bigger budget. The internet gave smaller players new asymmetry. It let them punch above their weight. It made entrepreneurial speed more valuable.

That's why I didn't see the internet as a fax machine. I saw it as a weapon for the underdog.

And that's exactly why I care so much about AI agents now. Because I'm seeing the same misread all over again.

Today, most businesses are treating AI the way businesses in the early 1990s treated the internet. They're translating a structural shift through the smallest possible metaphor. They think AI is a faster search engine. A better copywriter. A smarter chatbot. A meeting summarizer. A way to write emails and social posts a little faster.

That's not wrong. It's just too small. It's email-equals-fax thinking all over again.

If your understanding of AI begins and ends with content generation, you're looking at the surface and missing the architecture. The deeper shift isn't that machines can generate text. The deeper shift is that software is moving from passive tool to active worker.

That's a different world.

A passive tool waits for instructions. A spreadsheet doesn't wake up and monitor the business. A CRM doesn't think. Traditional software sits there until a human pushes buttons.

Agentic systems are different. They observe, reason, draft, route, monitor, escalate, coordinate, and act within boundaries. Not magic. Not full autonomy across everything. But something much more important in practical business terms: a new layer of labor.

That changes the design of a company. Not just the marketing. Not just the content team. Not just the help desk. The company.

That's why I get impatient when I hear business owners say, "Yes, we use AI. We use it to help with Instagram captions."

Fine. Better than nothing. But that's not the game. That's the equivalent of discovering the internet and saying, "This will be useful for sending product sheets faster than fax." Technically true. Strategically tiny.

The entrepreneurs who win major shifts are usually the ones who understand the scale of the change before the interface makes it obvious. They don't wait for cultural consensus. They study the direction, not just the current form.

That's what "twice ahead" means.

It means seeing the present more accurately than the crowd sees it. Not perfectly. More accurately. It means recognizing that the current form of a breakthrough technology is usually the least impressive version you'll ever see. It means refusing to anchor your strategic thinking to today's clunky interface. It means asking what this becomes after three, five, seven iterations of improvement—and understanding that when a new capability starts compounding, the pace catches people off guard.

The internet did that. AI will do it faster.

There's another reason people miss shifts like this, and it rarely gets discussed honestly. New technologies threaten status. If a new technology means a young outsider can do what used to require years of institutional positioning, the people who benefited from the old system have every incentive to minimize it. They call the new thing overhyped, amateur, dangerous, unserious, unproven. Sometimes consciously. Often not.

Some of those criticisms are partially true. Early versions are messy, overhyped, uneven. They can be dangerous when misused. The market attracts grifters. That happened online too—spam, junk, ugly websites, unserious operators, absurd claims. None of that meant the internet itself was small. It meant the gate had opened and human nature had arrived quickly.

The same thing is happening with AI. Hype everywhere. Nonsense everywhere. People pretending they built systems when they really just wrote a clever prompt. Executives talking about transformation without changing anything operationally. Marketers selling magic beans.

That doesn't prove AI is overblown. It proves the signal is buried under noise, which is normal at the beginning of every wave.

The trick is learning to separate immature implementation from immature potential. Most people fail at this. They conclude that because the average use of a technology is shallow, the technology itself must be shallow. They confuse the user with the capability. They confuse the current packaging with the actual underlying shift.

That's why the crowd is usually late. Not because the truth was unavailable. Because the truth was inconvenient.

Living through the commercial internet era gave me scar tissue most people don't have. I know what it feels like to watch a world-changing capability get dismissed as a novelty. I know what it feels like to build while the broader market is still debating whether the thing matters. I also know something else: being early is not enough by itself.

You don't get rewarded just for being right before other people. You get rewarded for building the right infrastructure while other people are still arguing.

Plenty of people were "right" about the internet in a vague sense. Far fewer turned that belief into domains, hosting, software, customer relationships, education, systems, and market position. Belief without execution is just prediction. The advantage comes from turning early pattern recognition into practical operating assets.

Today, when I look at AI, I'm not asking whether the tools can write a decent email. That's the wrong level of analysis. I'm asking what happens when every business can deploy a digital workforce of specialized agents across research, monitoring, drafting, customer communication, operational support, reporting, follow-up, and process management.

What happens when a five-person company can operate with the capability of a fifty-person company? When an entrepreneur with the right architecture can out-execute a much larger competitor? When service businesses stop being constrained by purely human throughput? When knowledge, judgment support, and process execution become available on demand, twenty-four hours a day, at a cost structure that keeps compressing?

Those are internet-scale questions.

That's why I don't see the current AI moment as a nice productivity trend. I see it as the early construction phase of a new business operating model.

And just like the internet, it won't unfold evenly. Some industries will move faster. Some will resist longer. Some will adopt surface-level AI and tell themselves they innovated. Others will redesign workflows, teams, economics, and decision architecture from the ground up. Some founders will use AI as decoration. Others will use it to build companies that are structurally harder to compete with.

The gap between those groups is going to get wide. Wider than most people think.

If you're reading this as an entrepreneur, founder, or executive, here's the important point: you don't need perfect certainty to act. You need enough pattern recognition to stop underestimating what's happening.

In the early internet era, not everyone needed to predict every winner. But the people who understood the direction could still make good bets. They could claim domain real estate. They could learn the mechanics. They could build lists. They could establish digital presence. They could reduce dependency on older channels. They could develop fluency before the rest of the market woke up.

The same principle applies now. You don't need omniscience. You need posture. A posture of curiosity, urgency, experimentation, and structural thinking.

Most people won't adopt that posture because it asks too much of them psychologically. It asks them to admit that their current understanding may be too small. It asks them to step into ambiguity. It asks them to move before consensus makes the decision feel safe.

That's why pioneer windows never stay open long. Once the crowd can see the value clearly, the easy asymmetry is gone.

That's what I mean when I say I've seen this movie before. I don't mean history repeats in identical form. I mean the human reaction repeats. The institutional blindness. The expert dismissal. The mislabeling. The tendency to confuse the first crude version with the final implication.

And the opportunity repeats too.

Right now, there's still time to be early in a meaningful way. Not first in some technical sense. Early enough to redesign your company while competitors are still treating AI as an accessory. Early enough to build internal systems before the market standardizes. Early enough to gain fluency while others are still attending webinars and forwarding articles to each other.

That's not a theoretical advantage. That becomes better margins, better responsiveness, better decision support, better customer experience, better speed, better use of human talent, and eventually, better enterprise value.

That's where this book is going. Not into abstraction. Not into hype. Into build.

Because once you see that the current AI moment is being misread the same way the internet was misread, a more uncomfortable question shows up: Who is most likely to see the shift clearly before everyone else does?

In my experience, it's usually not the insiders.

It's the outsiders.

And that's where we go next.

Chapter 2

The Outsider's Edge

I learned computers from the outside of the glass.

That's not a metaphor.

As a teenager in Germany, I couldn't afford a computer, so I'd go to department stores and computer shops and wait for them to open. I wanted to be first to the demo machines before anyone else claimed them. Usually it was a Commodore 64 or an Atari. I'd sit there writing programs in BASIC, sometimes a little assembler, trying to squeeze as much learning as I could out of borrowed time on someone else's machine.

I studied COBOL by reading books in the university library. Not because I was enrolled. Because I wanted in.

That matters more than people think.

When you come in through the side door, you notice things the insiders miss. You don't inherit their assumptions. You don't absorb their limits. You're too busy figuring out how the thing works to care about the politics around it.

That outsider position shaped my life long before I had any success. It shaped how I saw computers. It shaped how I saw America. It shaped how I saw business. And it's one of the main reasons I was early to the commercial internet when most people still thought email was a fancy fax machine.

It's also why I believe the next dangerous wave of competition in nearly every industry won't come from the people who've been in that industry the longest. It will come from the people standing slightly outside it.

The immigrant sees what the citizen takes for granted. The self-taught builder sees what the credentialed expert overlooks. The industry-crosser sees where the margins, the friction, and the waste are hiding—because he's not emotionally attached to the old way.

That's the real subject of this chapter. Not my biography. Strategy.

I came to the United States in 1986, to New York, at twenty-one years old. The original plan was modeling, not technology. That didn't work out. I spent about two years as an assistant to a fashion photographer before moving to Florida.

That period wasn't glamorous. It was instructive.

When you arrive in a new country with limited English, very little money, and no institutional advantage, you learn that the world doesn't owe you orientation. Nobody hands you a map. You watch. You listen. You adapt. You become very sensitive to how systems actually work—because survival depends on it.

That's one of the great hidden strengths of outsiders. We study reality faster. Insiders can afford to rely on convention for a long time. Outsiders usually can't.

By 1989, I'd scraped together $5,000 to start a carpet cleaning business—from a newspaper ad that brought in exactly two responses. That was enough. I took the shot. I bought an IBM-compatible machine at Office Depot for about $1,000. It had 1 MB of RAM, roughly a 10 MB hard drive, and a modem.

By today's standards, it was primitive. To me, it was a gateway.

That modem changed the trajectory of my life. I started connecting to GEnie and CompuServe—text-based online services that were slow, clunky, and not remotely intuitive. No polished interface. No beautiful design. You had to want to be there.

I wanted to be there.

I didn't arrive through a computer science department or a venture-backed startup or Silicon Valley. I arrived through curiosity, hunger, and a modem attached to a basic machine paid for by a gritty little service business.

For all practical purposes, I was self-taught.

That outsider path gave me three advantages I didn't fully appreciate at the time.

First, I was willing to learn ugly things.

That sounds small, but it matters. Early technology is almost always ugly. Awkward, slow, incomplete, badly explained. The insiders who dominate an existing industry usually look at it and dismiss it—it's not yet elegant enough to threaten the current model. Outsiders tolerate the ugliness because they're focused on capability, not polish.

I saw this in the early online services. I saw it again when the web arrived. And I see it right now with AI agents.

Most people judge a breakthrough too early by the user experience of the current version. They say, "It hallucinates." They say, "It still needs supervision." They say, "It's not reliable enough."

All of that may be true in part. It's also beside the point.

The better question: what direction is it moving, and what does that make possible for the people who start building now?

Outsiders ask that question because they're not measuring the new technology against the comfort of the current system. They're measuring it against the possibility of creating an advantage.

Second, I wasn't trapped inside industry dogma.

When I moved deeper into internet infrastructure in the mid-1990s, I wasn't burdened by a legacy worldview that said the old gatekeepers had to remain the gatekeepers. That gave me the freedom to build things other people weren't even attempting. I coined the term "autoresponder" in 1994 because I was already thinking in systems. I wasn't asking how to send one email. I was thinking about how to create a sequence, a response mechanism, a machine that worked while you slept.

That's outsider thinking. Not because outsiders are smarter. Because they're less loyal to the inherited boundaries.

In 1995, I built the first web-based domain registration service. The commercial internet still looked small and uncertain to most people. Many businesses didn't understand why they needed a website, let alone a domain strategy. But I wasn't looking at the world through their level of adoption. I was looking at where the infrastructure needed to go.

That's another outsider trait: you're more willing to build for the future customer than the present consensus.

Consensus is almost always late. It feels safe because many people share it. It's usually expensive for exactly the same reason. By the time everyone agrees, the easy upside is gone.

Third, I'd developed a kind of entrepreneurial pattern recognition that came from necessity.

When you start with very little, you get obsessed with leverage. You have to. You can't outspend the market. You can't hire your way out of inefficiency. You can't cover bad decisions with excess capital. So you become highly sensitive to tools, systems, and business models that let a small operator do the work of a much larger one.

That instinct drove me in the internet era. It drove me later in real estate. It drives me now with AI.

When I entered real estate, I was coming in with an outsider's lens again. I hadn't spent twenty years becoming emotionally attached to the way things had always been done. I saw a business full of friction, paperwork, delays, weak systems, low operational discipline, and a lot of accepted inefficiency.

Most insiders stop seeing friction after a while. It blends into the wallpaper. They call it "just part of the business."

That phrase should terrify you.

"Just part of the business" is where margin goes to die. It's where waste hides. It's where outsiders find openings.

I built in real estate the same way I built in technology: by looking for structural weakness that insiders had normalized. That mindset led to paperless systems early. It led to large-scale processing operations. It led to rethinking how brokerages could be structured. It eventually led to building a title company with the explicit goal of using AI to redesign how work gets done.

The outsider's edge isn't about rebellion for its own sake. It's about freedom from unnecessary obedience.

A useful outsider doesn't reject convention because it's conventional. He rejects convention when it stops making economic sense. The best outsiders aren't anti-industry. They're anti-complacency. They don't hate expertise. They hate stale expertise. They don't ignore history. They refuse to let history become a cage.

If you're reading this as a founder, executive, or operator, here's the uncomfortable truth: your biggest threat in the AI era may not be your most obvious competitor.

It may be a smaller, faster, less credentialed operator who's willing to redesign the workflow you've been tolerating for years. It may be somebody from outside your category entirely. Somebody who doesn't know your industry "well enough" to respect its sacred cows.

That's often exactly the person you should worry about.

Outsiders bring fresh economic eyes. They ask why five people are touching the same file. They ask why knowledge is trapped in inboxes. They ask why a business earning millions still runs on tribal knowledge and heroic follow-up. Insiders hear those questions as naive. I hear them as expensive.

Regulated industries are especially vulnerable right now because many have built their identity around complexity. Legal, healthcare, financial services, title, insurance, compliance-heavy operations—all of them contain layers of work that were historically difficult to coordinate. Because that complexity was real, the surrounding human process became sacred.

But once AI agents can handle parts of the coordination—routing, drafting, tracking, monitoring, escalation, memory—some of that sacred process stops being an asset and starts becoming drag.

The outsider sees drag faster. Not because he knows more about the regulations. Because he knows less about the rituals.

This is one of the main reasons I'm so bullish on agent-powered businesses. I'm not approaching this as a pure technologist. I'm approaching it as someone who has spent decades moving between industries, building in periods of transition, and noticing the same pattern.

The incumbents almost always underestimate the people who aren't fully socialized into the incumbent system.

That happened in the early internet. Many established businesses treated it like an accessory—something for the marketing department to experiment with while the real business continued elsewhere. That was a catastrophic misread. The internet wasn't an accessory. It became infrastructure.

AI will follow a similar path, but the shift cuts deeper.

This time it's not only external—how customers find you, contact you, buy from you. It's internal. It changes how the company itself thinks, remembers, routes, executes, monitors, and scales.

That makes the outsider's advantage even more dangerous.

A founder coming from outside your industry can now use AI to compensate for missing organizational depth while building it. He can deploy agents as researchers, assistants, monitors, and workflow engines. He can create a level of operating discipline that once required layers of management. Not perfect discipline. Not finished discipline. But enough to become a real threat much sooner.

That compresses the timeline.

In the old days, challenging an entrenched industry meant you needed more people, more office infrastructure, more training capacity, and more managerial overhead before you even looked serious. Now a lean team with the right systems can punch far above its weight.

That's why so many incumbents are underestimating what's coming. They're still asking, "Can AI write a decent email?"

The sharper question: "What happens when a smaller competitor builds an execution architecture that lets three people operate like thirty?"

That's not a gimmick. That's a strategic threat.

I want to make this personal for a moment.

My life forced me into outsider mode early. I wasn't born into stability. I didn't come into business through elite networks. I didn't arrive in America with a polished plan. I built from edges, not from centers.

At the time, that felt like a disadvantage. In many ways, it was. But it trained me to be comfortable without belonging to the dominant framework. It trained me to look for openings instead of approval. It trained me to trust direct observation over social consensus.

That skill is enormously valuable when the world is changing.

When an industry is stable, insiders win because the game is defined and they know the rules. When an industry is shifting, outsiders gain power because they're less attached to the old rulebook.

Self-taught people learn by assembling fragments. They reverse-engineer. They test. They improvise. They develop a bias toward function over form. They're less impressed by institutional packaging and more interested in what the thing can actually do.

That mindset is perfect for frontier moments.

The same is true of immigrants. An immigrant is often running two operating systems at once—the visible system of the new country and the internal translation layer required to survive inside it. That dual awareness produces unusual strategic clarity. You start to notice which behaviors are cultural, which are structural, which are necessary, and which are just habit wearing a suit.

And industry-crossers carry questions into every new field that insiders may no longer think to ask. Why does this process require so many handoffs? Why do we tolerate this delay? Why is this knowledge not systematized? Why is this still manual?

Those are outsider questions. Those are also builder questions. Ask them long enough and you stop merely participating in an industry and start redesigning it.

Now let me say something some people won't like.

Being an insider is overrated when the environment is changing quickly.

Deep expertise still matters. Domain knowledge matters. Relationships matter. Judgment matters. I'm not arguing otherwise.

But expertise becomes dangerous when it hardens into identity.

The minute your expertise starts telling you why the next shift won't matter, your expertise is decaying into nostalgia.

I've watched this too many times. The people most certain the internet would remain limited were often the ones with the most to lose if it expanded. The people most certain traditional real estate models didn't need redesign were the ones who'd built careers inside those models. The people most certain AI agents will remain toys are often evaluating them from inside organizations optimized for a labor-heavy past.

They're not neutral observers. Neither are you. Neither am I.

That's why strategic self-awareness matters. You have to ask yourself: where am I seeing clearly, and where am I defending the version of the world that made me successful?

That question separates builders from protectors. Protectors defend the existing structure. Builders study what the structure is becoming.

To stay twice ahead, you don't need to become an outsider in the literal sense. You don't need to immigrate, switch industries, or teach yourself programming on a demo machine in a department store.

But you do need to cultivate outsider vision.

That means stepping outside your industry's default assumptions. Bringing in people who ask annoying but intelligent questions. Rewarding observation over hierarchy. Examining your workflows as if you were trying to attack your own business model. Assuming that whatever your industry treats as "just the way it works" is a candidate for redesign.

And it means paying close attention to the people your industry is most tempted to dismiss.

Those may be the people building the future version of your business while you're still polishing the old one.

From the kid standing outside the computer store to the immigrant decoding America to the entrepreneur dialing into text-based services through a $1,000 computer and a modem—my path was never the neat, insider path.

Good. That was the edge.

The edge was never credentials. The edge was distance. Distance from the accepted story. Distance from the inherited limit. Distance from the expert consensus that usually arrives right after the real opportunity has already gone to work.

That's the opportunity now with AI. The market is still treating most of it like a feature set. A writing tool. A design tool. A smarter search box. Useful, but contained.

That's how markets behave early. They interpret a structural shift through the lens of the current category.

The real shift is not from bad tools to better tools. It's from isolated tools to agentic systems. From one-off outputs to ongoing execution. From software you use to digital workers you manage. From labor-heavy organizations to human-led, agent-powered companies.

That's where this book is going next.

The outsider sees the opening first. But seeing it isn't enough. You also have to understand the nature of the shift.

And most people—even now—are still confusing a tool with an agent.

Chapter 3

From Tool to Agent: The Shift Most People Are Missing

Most people still think AI is a smarter search box with good manners. That is the mistake.

They open ChatGPT, ask a question, get a decent answer, maybe have it rewrite an email or summarize a report, and walk away thinking they're using the future. They're not wrong. They're just standing at the entrance.

The real shift starts when AI stops being something you ask and starts becoming something you assign.

That difference sounds small when you say it fast. It's not. It's the difference between a calculator and a bookkeeper. Between software you click and work that moves while you sleep. Between a clever assistant on your screen and a digital workforce that can carry part of the load of a company.

I've seen this kind of misunderstanding before.

In the early internet era, most people reduced the whole thing to one narrow use case. Email would replace fax machines. Websites were digital brochures. A lot of smart people looked at the internet and saw a slightly better version of something they already understood.

That is exactly what is happening with AI right now.

If your entire concept of AI is "it helps me think" or "it helps me write," you're looking at the first inning of a much bigger game.

What matters is not just that AI can generate language. What matters is that AI is becoming capable of carrying out work. And once you see that, the economics change. The org chart changes. The companies of the next decade separate themselves from the ones that spend it catching up.

The adoption curve is fairly clear.

First, people use AI to ask questions and get advice.

Second, they move into what I'd call co-work mode. They instruct the system to take actions. Sort these files. Draft these replies. Update this KPI sheet. Run this task every morning. Alert me if something fails.

Third—and this is the part most people don't fully see—you move into autonomous agents. Not fantasy robots. Not science fiction. I mean role-based agents with a defined job, tools, memory, guardrails, escalation rules, and human oversight. A specialist for research. Another for operations. Another for quality control. Another for monitoring. Each one narrow enough to be reliable, useful, and trainable.

That third stage is where the model changes from tool to worker. And once that happens, you're no longer talking about productivity tricks. You're talking about a new operating system for business.

The first stage is where most people still live. There's nothing wrong with it. If a business owner has never used AI, I'd rather see them use it badly than ignore it completely. Ask it questions. Have it clean up rough writing. Use it to pressure-test your thinking. That matters because it changes behavior and gets people comfortable.

But let's be honest. That stage is still cognitive support. You're thinking, the AI is helping. You're deciding, the AI is assisting. You're moving the work, the AI is commenting from the passenger seat.

That's why so many people use AI every day and still haven't changed their business in any meaningful way. They feel more informed. They're not yet more scalable. They still have the same bottlenecks. They just have slightly prettier documents coming out of them.

The second stage is more interesting. This is where AI crosses the line from adviser to actor. You're not just asking for ideas. You're asking the system to do something. Run a recurring report. Monitor an inbox. Classify incoming documents. Flag exceptions. Summarize yesterday's activity and tell you what needs attention.

That's not full autonomy, but it's real work. The machine is no longer sitting next to you talking. It's moved onto the floor.

This stage matters because it rewires how a founder thinks. The question changes from "What can AI tell me?" to "What can I hand off?"

That is a much better question.

Once you start thinking that way, you see the company differently. You stop seeing isolated tasks and start seeing workflows. You notice how much of the day is made up of routing, checking, drafting, monitoring, copying, comparing, chasing, formatting, following up, and packaging information for the next person.

Most businesses are drowning in that kind of work. Not hard work—repetitive work. Not genius work—coordination work. Not creative work—throughput work. And that is exactly where AI becomes dangerous in the best possible sense.

Because once a system can reliably handle some of that work, even under supervision, the founder sees something bigger than savings or convenience. Capacity.

That's when the third stage comes into focus. This is the stage I'm working toward with OpenClaw.

I want to be precise here, because hype destroys credibility.

OpenClaw is not a polished commercial product. Cloud Title is not fully AI-automated. I have not replaced my human team with agents, and anyone claiming that kind of overnight transformation either doesn't understand real operations or is selling theater. What is true is that I'm actively building a multi-agent operating environment, and it's already far enough along to show me the shape of what's coming.

I'm building agents with specific roles. Some handle research. Some handle engineering. Some handle content. Some handle monitoring and synthesis. They operate with instructions, memory, tools, and boundaries. They can handle parts of a process independently and then escalate, report back, or wait for approval where appropriate.

It's still early. There's friction. Trust issues to solve. Governance questions. Orchestration problems. Sometimes a five-minute task turns into a forty-minute debugging session because one tool call fails or one instruction is too vague.

Good. That's what real building looks like.

And even in the messy middle, the strategic implication is already obvious: once you can create a role-based agent that handles meaningful work inside guardrails, you're no longer dealing with software in the traditional sense. You're dealing with labor.

Digital labor.

That phrase makes some people uncomfortable, but I think it's accurate. Not because AI is a person—it isn't. Not because human judgment no longer matters—it matters more than ever. But because the economic role is starting to resemble labor, not software. Software waits for clicks. A worker has responsibilities. Software sits there until you open it. A worker has a queue. Software gives you functions. A worker owns outcomes within a defined role.

Think about your best employee. Every founder has one. The person who holds everything together. Fast. Sharp. Reliable. Handles exceptions. Protects the business from chaos.

Now imagine I tell you to grow your company a hundred times. How do you hundred-x that person?

You don't. You can't clone a top human performer without hiring, training, waiting, managing, and hoping. Human scale is linear, slow, expensive, and fragile.

An AI agent that's been properly trained for a narrow role, given the right instructions, connected to the right tools, and wrapped in the right controls? You can copy it. Five times. Fifty times. That doesn't mean all copies should run wild. It means the upper bound has changed. The old limit was headcount. The new limit is system design.

For years, scale meant recruiting, training, management layers, and office politics. Now an increasing share of scale comes from clarity. Clear roles. Clear instructions. Clear escalation rules. Clear quality standards. Clear system architecture. The companies that know how to design work are going to beat the companies that only know how to hire for it.

That doesn't eliminate people. It upgrades the premium on the right people.

The founder who understands judgment, trust, service, brand, ethics, and strategy becomes more valuable, not less. The operator who can define processes cleanly becomes more valuable. The manager who can create scoreboards, exception handling, and accountability becomes more valuable.

But the company that insists every piece of repetitive work must be done by a human just because that's how it's always been done? That company is going to get buried.

This is why the real AI story is structural, not incremental.

Incremental: write emails faster, summarize meetings faster, brainstorm faster. Structural: redesign how work enters the company, gets routed, gets checked, gets completed, gets monitored, gets escalated, and gets improved over time. One is a feature upgrade. The other is a business model upgrade.

And the earlier you see that, the earlier you stop buying toys when you should be redesigning operations.

Let me make this concrete. In a title company, think about how much activity has nothing to do with high-level legal judgment and everything to do with intake, document handling, monitoring, exception spotting, follow-up, cross-checking, and status movement. A human still needs to make critical calls and protect the client experience. But a large share of the surrounding motion is process.

The same is true in real estate. In law. In lending, logistics, healthcare administration, recruiting, and almost every service business I can think of. High-value human judgment sits in the middle, buried under layers of checking, chasing, routing, assembling, and reminding.

Agents should be narrow before they become broad. A good agent doesn't need to be a genius philosopher. It needs to be reliable at a defined job. If an agent can monitor an inbox, classify incoming messages, prepare a first-pass response, and escalate the outliers, that alone removes a surprising amount of drag. If another can run a daily KPI pull, compare it to prior periods, and surface anomalies before the owner even asks, that's not a gimmick. That's operational advantage.

And there's another edge most people haven't processed: agents don't care what time it is. They don't forget to run the checklist because three other requests came in. A well-designed agent watches, checks, compares, routes, and reports with a consistency most organizations have never actually achieved.

This is where outsiders keep winning. The incumbent sees AI as an add-on. The outsider sees it as a chance to rebuild the machine. A smaller, hungrier company can take one core workflow, redesign it around agents, measure the output, improve the controls, and then do it again. That's how a company becomes AI-native. Not by announcing it. By rebuilding itself one function at a time.

That's what happened in the internet era too. The companies that won were often not the ones with the best legacy assets. They were the ones willing to rethink what the business even was.

Once agents are part of the labor system, management itself changes. You don't "prompt" an agent the way you prompt a chatbot. You define a role. Assign responsibility. Set rules. Specify tools. Determine what good looks like. Create escalation paths. Monitor performance. Improve the system. That is management—a different kind, but management nonetheless.

And this is where a lot of founders will hit a wall. They want AI to be magical, but they don't want to do the design work. They want autonomy without architecture. Output without governance. Scale without discipline.

That's not how this works. A badly designed agent creates noise at scale just as a badly designed team creates bureaucracy at scale. An undisciplined company with AI doesn't become brilliant. It becomes chaotic faster.

So I'm not arguing that every business should unleash a swarm of autonomous agents on Monday morning and hope for the best. I'm arguing something more serious: start seeing your company through the lens of agent-compatible work.

Where is the repetition? The routing? The monitoring? The first-pass drafting? The follow-up? The task that happens every day with slight variation but the same basic shape?

That's where your future digital workforce begins.

Over time, this points toward increasingly autonomous organizations. I believe we're moving toward companies where a growing percentage of operational activity is handled by agent teams, with humans providing vision, values, boundaries, approvals, and judgment where judgment actually matters. There will be founder-guided systems that can identify issues, surface opportunities, execute approved tasks, monitor results, and improve the process with less and less direct intervention.

But let me say it clearly: autonomous does not mean unsupervised stupidity.

The point isn't to remove humans from the loop because humans are unnecessary. The point is to remove humans from the wrong parts of the loop. A lot of work never needed human brilliance. It only needed human availability. That distinction is going to matter enormously in the years ahead.

What excites me most is the asymmetry. A founder with the right systems can now build capabilities that used to require a much bigger organization. Research capacity, monitoring capacity, drafting capacity, analytical capacity, engineering support, operational support—all within reach of a lean team that would have been locked out of those capabilities a few years ago.

That's not just efficiency. That's strategic power.

The next generation of breakout companies may not look big from the outside. They'll look lean, focused, and fast. But under the hood, they'll have a labor model their competitors don't understand.

If you miss this distinction, you'll keep using AI like a smart intern you chat with from time to time. If you see it clearly, you'll start redesigning your business around roles, workflows, oversight, and scale.

You'll stop asking, "What can ChatGPT help me write?"

You'll start asking, "What part of my company can an agent own?"

That question leads directly to the next one: if agents are going to own more of the repetition, routing, drafting, monitoring, and execution—what exactly should humans own?

The future is not human versus machine. It's human-led, agent-powered.

And that is where we go next.

Part II:
The Framework

Chapter 4

Human-Led, Agent-Powered

A lot of people hear the phrase AI agents and immediately jump to the wrong conclusion.

They picture some fully autonomous machine enterprise where humans disappear, decisions get outsourced, and the founder becomes a spectator in his own company.

That is not what I am building. And it is not what I think smart business owners should build.

What I want is a human-led business with far more capability than a traditional company of its size should be able to have. I want experienced people doing the work that requires experience, judgment, trust, and vision. And I want agents handling the growing mountain of repetitive, structured, routeable work that quietly eats the life out of a company.

I see founders getting this wrong in both directions every day.

One side is drunk on automation fantasy. They think every person is a cost center, every workflow can be handed to a machine, and governance is some annoying detail you worry about later. They confuse possibility with readiness. They talk like replacing humans is the point.

It is not.

The other side treats AI like a toy. They let people use ChatGPT to write

emails and polish social posts, then pat themselves on the back for "adopting AI."
Meanwhile the actual operating model of the company remains unchanged. Same
bottlenecks. Same overloaded managers. Same missed handoffs. Same human
beings wasting good judgment on low-value administrative work.

The right model sits in the middle, and it is much more powerful than either
extreme.

Human-led. Agent-powered.

I have become more convinced of this by doing the work, not by watching
demos.

At Cloud Title, we are still early in the transformation. We are not some magical fully autonomous title company, and I have no interest in pretending otherwise. We use Qualia as our core production platform. We have adopted Qualia
Clear. We are building automation around the edges — lien search automation,
transaction coordination, agent follow-up, internal support. Some things work.
Some things are promising. Some things are messy. That is real life.

Inside OpenClaw, I am running a live experiment in what an agent-powered
operating environment looks like. Not in theory. In practice. Multiple agents
with distinct roles, different responsibilities, different trust levels, different handoffs. Human direction still matters. Human review still matters. But the throughput, coverage, and continuity you can create starts to change dramatically once
the work is structured properly.

The first lesson from all of this is simple: the future is not AI instead of people.
The future is the right people, supported by the right agents, inside the right
system.

If you are a founder, you need to stop asking, "How do I use AI?"

The better question is, "What should remain human in my company, and what
should be agent-handled by design?"

That is an operating question. And operating questions change companies.

When I lived through the early commercial internet, people made the same
mistake. They assumed the internet was either a novelty or a total replacement for
everything. Both readings were wrong. The internet did not eliminate the need

for real businesses. It rewarded the companies that redesigned themselves around a new capability. AI agents are not just a better software feature. They are a new layer of labor — digital labor. And once you understand that, you stop treating agents like glorified chat boxes and start treating them like role-based capacity.

But before we get to economics, we have to get the leadership model right. No serious company can be built on the idea that machines should own judgment.

Humans own vision.

A business does not exist to process tasks. It exists to pursue a direction. Somebody has to decide where the company is going, what game it is playing, which risks are acceptable, and what tradeoffs it is willing to make. No agent should be deciding the mission of a company. It can support it and accelerate it, but mission is human territory.

Humans own judgment.

This is where a lot of bad AI conversations go off the rails. People talk about intelligence as if all intelligence is the same. It is not. Pattern recognition is not judgment. Prediction is not judgment. Speed is not judgment. Judgment lives in ambiguity. It weighs second-order consequences. It understands context that is not in the prompt. It knows when a technically correct answer is still the wrong move.

In a regulated business, that matters even more. In title, you are not just moving documents around. You are dealing with money, timelines, legal obligations, emotional clients, lenders, agents, underwriters, and the possibility of error at very expensive moments. A machine can flag, route, summarize, and draft. But the accountability for the final call still belongs to a person.

Humans own trust.

A client may appreciate automation. They may even prefer the speed and fewer mistakes it creates. But when something sensitive happens — the deal is at risk, an exception appears, emotions rise — they want to know who is responsible. They want a name, a voice, and a person with authority. That is not going away.

Humans own ethics.

An agent can follow rules. It cannot bear moral responsibility. A company still has to decide how aggressive it wants to be, how it handles gray areas, and how it balances speed with safety. Those are leadership decisions, not software settings.

Humans own the final decision.

I am not saying every human must touch every task. I am saying every business needs well-defined points where responsibility lands with a human being who can approve, override, escalate, or stop. In a well-built company, agents increase the number of things that are ready for decision. Humans still make the important ones.

That is one half of the model. The second half is just as important: agents should own far more work than most companies currently let them.

Agents should own repetition.

Anything that happens over and over, in a recognizable pattern, with known inputs and expected outputs, should immediately get your attention. How many times is your staff retyping the same information, checking the same status, chasing the same missing detail, drafting the same basic follow-up? That is where agent power becomes obvious.

Agents should own routing.

A shocking amount of business friction is not difficult work — it is misplaced work. The wrong person gets the issue. The right person gets it too late. Nobody knows who owns the next step. Messages sit. Requests pile up. Follow-up depends on memory instead of system. Agents can watch for events, classify inputs, trigger the next action, assign tasks, summarize context, and move work to the right person with a consistency that many teams simply do not have.

Agents should own drafting.

Drafting is not deciding. Most business communication does not need to begin from a blank page. Most update emails, status reports, exception notes, and research memos can start with an agent. Not end there — start there. That alone changes the cadence of a business.

Agents should own monitoring.

Human beings are not built to watch twenty things at once all day without fatigue or distraction. Agents are. They can monitor inboxes, workflows, deadlines, status changes, exception conditions, missing data, and incomplete handoffs that no one on the team has time to watch consistently. A monitored company is a different company. Problems get seen earlier. Small failures stay small. Bottlenecks stop hiding.

Agents should own continuity.

Human teams forget. They get interrupted. They change priorities. They leave. They miss a note from two weeks ago that matters today. A well-designed agent layer can preserve context, keep projects warm, surface prior decisions, and maintain continuity across longer timelines better than many conventional teams do.

Once you see this clearly, the operating model starts to sharpen. Humans should spend more of their time on work that deserves human bandwidth. Agents should absorb more of the work that does not.

In practice, most companies are built backward. The founder is buried in follow-up. The best operator is drowning in status checks. The person who should be solving exceptions is typing routine emails. The person who should be building relationships is updating spreadsheets. Everyone says they are overwhelmed — and of course they are. They are using expensive human judgment to perform low-value coordination work because the company has no digital labor layer.

The solution is not just "use AI more." The solution is to redesign who owns what.

When I look at a workflow now, I ask five questions. Does this step require human trust? Does it require human judgment? Does it involve ethical or legal accountability? Does it happen often enough that system beats memory? And if it disappeared from a human's day, would that person become more valuable somewhere else?

If the answer is yes to trust, judgment, or accountability, a human needs to own the decision point. If the answer is yes to frequency, structure, and recoverable error, an agent should probably handle more of it. And often the answer is not all-or-nothing: first pass by agent, second pass by human. Monitoring by agent, intervention by human. Drafting by agent, approval by human. Routing by agent, execution by human.

This is where intelligent companies will separate from sloppy ones. They will stop thinking in binary terms and start designing layers.

Agents should be first on repetitive work. Humans should be first on consequential decisions. Agents should prepare the work. Humans should own the outcome.

That is the framework.

It is also the answer to one of the biggest emotional objections to this entire shift: What happens to people?

Good people become more valuable in an agent-powered company, not less. But their value moves. The person who was once valuable because they could personally keep ten plates spinning becomes even more valuable if they can design and supervise a system where a hundred plates spin with help from agents. The employee whose main contribution was manually moving information from one place to another is at risk — that is just being honest. But the employee who can exercise judgment, manage exceptions, strengthen customer trust, and collaborate with agents is entering a much stronger position.

The future does not belong to companies that simply cut headcount and call it strategy. It belongs to companies that upgrade the level at which their people operate.

In a human-only company, scale is mostly a hiring problem. In a human-led, agent-powered company, scale becomes a design problem. Design scales better.

That does not mean it is easy. In some ways it is harder at first, because you have to be explicit about things most companies leave vague. You have to define roles. Decide trust boundaries. Specify when an agent can act, when it must ask, when it must escalate, and what counts as success. You have to be honest about your workflows.

That is uncomfortable for companies that have survived on heroics. Heroic cultures sound impressive until you realize they are usually just undocumented systems held together by memory and effort. Agents expose that. They force clarity. If an agent cannot reliably support a workflow, that often means the workflow itself is sloppy, contradictory, or tribal. That is useful information.

One of the hidden benefits of building with agents is that it forces a founder to become more precise about how the company actually works. Not how it should work on the org chart — how it really works. Where does intake come from? Who owns the next step? What triggers escalation? What information must exist before work proceeds? What happens if no one responds?

Those are leadership questions disguised as systems questions. And once you answer them, your company starts getting stronger even before the automation is perfect.

I have also found that trust with agents should be earned, not assumed.

You do not hire a new human team member and let them make unsupervised decisions on day one in sensitive areas of the business. You give them scoped responsibility. You define what good looks like. You test judgment. You review output. You expand trust gradually. Agents should be managed the same way. Start narrow. Give them a role, boundaries, inputs, and escalation rules. Let them prove reliability. Then widen the lane.

Trust calibration will become one of the defining management skills of the next decade. Some founders will be too timid — they will keep agents boxed into trivial tasks and never redesign the company enough to matter. Others will be too loose — they will over-delegate to systems they do not understand and pay for it in errors, compliance failures, or brand damage. The winners will know exactly where human review is non-negotiable, and exactly where agent execution should be aggressive.

That is what human-led actually means. It does not mean humans do everything. It means humans define the standard, own the judgment, and remain responsible for the outcome.

One more thing, because it gets lost in the hype: being human-led is not just a risk-control strategy. It is a value-creation strategy.

The real prize is not doing the same work cheaper. The real prize is building a company that can do better work, respond faster, maintain continuity, create more output, notice more signals, and operate with a level of capacity that used to require much larger payroll. That changes what kind of business you can build. It changes the size of problem you can take on. It changes the speed at which you can experiment. It changes the economics of service businesses, operating companies, agencies, brokerages, law firms, healthcare practices, and almost every other knowledge-driven organization.

This is not a software trend. It is a new management model. And management models change eras. Factories changed when machinery changed. Retail changed when distribution changed. Media changed when the internet changed. Knowledge businesses are about to change because labor itself is changing — not human labor disappearing, but digital labor arriving.

Founders who understand that early will stop organizing their companies as if the only capacity available is human time. The new company is led by people but expanded by agents. It has more awareness than its headcount suggests. More responsiveness than its org chart suggests. More consistency than its growth stage should normally allow.

That is what I mean by twice ahead. Not using a new tool before everyone else. Designing around a new reality before everyone else.

If you get this chapter right, you stop seeing AI as a clever assistant and start seeing it as a new operating layer. And once you see that, another question shows up immediately: if a company is going to be human-led and agent-powered, what does the org chart look like?

Chapter 5

The New Org Chart

M ost org charts are already obsolete. They just don't know it yet.

Walk into a typical company today and the boxes still look familiar. Owner. CEO. Operations manager. Assistant. Sales team. Marketing coordinator. Customer service. Maybe a few vendors and a handful of software subscriptions duct-taped together in the background. On paper, it looks clean. In reality, most businesses run on a chaotic mix of people, inboxes, apps, memory, interruptions, and heroic improvisation.

That was barely sustainable before AI. It'll be completely inadequate after it.

The next generation of companies won't be built around humans alone. They'll be built around a hybrid workforce: humans, software systems, and narrowly defined AI agents working together inside a designed structure.

That sentence matters, because most people still think about AI in the wrong shape. They imagine one magical super-assistant that does everything—one giant brain sitting in the middle of the company answering questions, writing copy, solving problems, and replacing half the payroll.

I don't believe that's how durable businesses will be built.

The future org chart isn't one super-agent. It's a coordinated team. Some of those team members are human. Some are software platforms. Some are AI agents. And each one needs a role, a lane, a level of authority, and a clearly defined handoff point.

When I look at the businesses that are going to pull ahead over the next few years, I don't ask, "Are they using AI?" That's too small a question now. I ask, "Have they redesigned how work is organized?" Because that's where the real advantage lives.

A company that uses AI to speed up a few tasks may get a temporary productivity bump. A company that redesigns its org chart around agents changes its operating model. Very different game.

In a legacy business, the org chart was a map of people. In an agent-powered business, the org chart becomes a map of responsibilities, decision rights, systems of record, and trust boundaries. Humans still matter—in fact, the better the AI gets, the more important it becomes to know where human judgment belongs. But now there are new kinds of roles inside the business: human leaders, human reviewers, software systems of record, orchestrators that route work, specialist agents that perform narrow functions, monitors that watch for exceptions, and task-specific execution agents handling research, drafting, QA, scheduling, and reporting.

If you don't design that structure deliberately, you'll get the worst of both worlds: confused staff, unreliable outputs, duplicated work, and a business that feels more complicated instead of more capable.

I'm seeing this firsthand in what I'm building right now.

Inside OpenClaw, I'm not trying to create one agent that does everything. I'm doing the opposite—assigning narrow roles. One agent is better suited for strategy. Another for research. Another for content. Another for technical implementation. Another for image generation. Another for infrastructure oversight. Even when two agents use the same underlying model, they're not the same worker. Their identities, instructions, responsibilities, and expected behavior are different.

That isn't a minor detail. That's the whole point.

At OpenClaw, we formalize this through identity files and role documents—in our case, files like SOUL.md and IDENTITY.md. You don't need those exact file names in your own business. But you need the discipline behind them.

An agent should know who it is, what it owns, what it doesn't own, when to escalate, what good work looks like, and where its output goes next.

Most entrepreneurs aren't used to thinking this way because they've been conditioned by software. Software is usually bought as a tool—you open it, click buttons, use features. Agents are different. Agents behave more like workers than like software, which means the management challenge changes.

You don't just configure an agent. You manage it. Not in the old sense of standing over its shoulder—in the structural sense. You define the role. You set the limits. You establish reporting lines. You determine the approval path. You calibrate trust. You measure the output. You revise the instructions. You decide what that agent is allowed to do independently and what still requires review.

A hybrid workforce only works when role design is precise.

That means you don't begin with the question, "What can AI do?" You begin with, "What role needs to exist inside this company?" Once you answer that, you can decide whether the role should be handled by a human, by software, by an agent, or by some combination of all three.

Take an executive assistant role. In a traditional company, that role includes scheduling, inbox triage, follow-up reminders, note consolidation, travel research, meeting preparation, and chasing loose ends. In a hybrid model, that same function gets distributed. Calendar software still manages the actual calendar. A human executive assistant still handles sensitive communications, relationship nuance, and judgment calls. But an AI assistant can prepare briefing notes, draft follow-ups, summarize meetings, organize information, and surface what needs attention before the human ever touches it.

The role doesn't disappear. It gets re-architected.

The same logic applies to marketing. A lot of entrepreneurs hear "AI marketing" and think of writing social media posts. That's far too narrow. A modern marketing function could include a human brand owner, a content strategist, a research agent that gathers source material, a copy agent that drafts long-form content, a design agent that creates visual assets, a publishing workflow tied to software platforms, and a review layer that ensures the final output is on-brand and factually sound.

Once you see the business through this lens—every function as a potential hybrid team—you stop thinking in terms of "using AI" and start thinking in terms of workforce architecture.

That's the mental shift this chapter is really about.

In the old world, scale meant adding headcount, outsourcing, or squeezing more productivity out of the same people. In the new world, scale can also mean adding highly specific agent roles that expand the capacity of the existing team without creating the same organizational drag. Not zero humans—fewer bottlenecks. Fewer people doing work that should never have required a person in the first place. A better match between human capability and human responsibility.

One of the most important roles in this new org chart is the orchestrator.

The orchestrator isn't the smartest agent in the system. It's the routing intelligence. Its job is to understand who should do what, in what order, under what conditions, and with what dependencies. In a human company, this role often gets performed informally by a founder, an operations manager, or a very competent assistant—someone who looks at the work coming in and mentally decides who touches it next.

That works when the team is small and the work is simple. It breaks when the system grows.

In an agent-powered environment, the orchestrator becomes one of the most valuable functions in the business because coordination itself becomes a source of advantage. It can receive an objective, break it into components, assign the right specialist to each part, collect outputs, and move the work toward completion. Without orchestration, you don't have a team. You have a collection of disconnected tools.

I see this clearly in a website build workflow. Say we're creating a new site. That project doesn't belong to one worker anymore. One agent takes the brief and creates the execution plan. Another drafts the copy. Another builds the site and publishes reviewable drafts. Another creates images or design components. Another does QA. A human still approves the design direction, edits the message, and makes final decisions. The system works because the roles are separated and coordinated.

That matters for quality, and it matters for speed. A generalist trying to do all of that alone usually creates drag. A coordinated specialist structure produces better output because each role can be optimized for one type of work.

One of the hidden truths of agent design: narrowness creates power.

The narrower the role, the better you can define standards. The better you define standards, the easier it becomes to evaluate output. The easier it becomes to evaluate output, the easier it becomes to trust the agent.

And trust is not a soft concept here. It's operational.

Every hybrid company will need some form of trust calibration. I think of this as a spectrum. At the lowest level, an agent can observe and report—summarize, flag, monitor, draft—but it doesn't execute anything final. At the next level, it can prepare actions for review: write the email, assemble the report, generate the draft response, but a human still approves before anything goes out. At a higher level, it can execute within defined boundaries—send internal notifications, update a project board, move items between stages, trigger pre-approved workflows. At the highest levels of trust, it can take actions that meaningfully affect operations or customers without human approval every time.

Most businesses should not start there. And frankly, most should not pretend they're there when they're not.

One reason I'm so focused on narrowly scoped agents is that it's much easier to assign trust when the role is precise. I may not trust a generic "operations agent" to run my business. I might trust a narrowly defined reporting agent to generate a daily dashboard, a monitoring agent to alert me when certain conditions occur, or a task-specific assistant to prepare client follow-up drafts.

Trust gets built with repetition, boundaries, and proof—not slogans.

The same principle applies to escalation. A good org chart doesn't just define who does the work. It defines what happens when the work falls outside normal conditions. Human companies already know this, even if they don't always document it well. If a processor finds something unusual in a file, it gets escalated. If a customer service rep encounters an upset client, it gets escalated. Agent systems need the same discipline.

An agent shouldn't be forced to pretend it knows what to do in every case. The better model is to define normal operations and exception handling separately. Inside its lane, the agent can move fast. Outside its lane, it stops, flags the issue, explains why it stopped, and routes the matter to the right human or supervising function.

One of the signs of a well-designed agent is not that it always acts. It's that it knows when not to.

That becomes critical in regulated, operational, or client-facing businesses. If you're in title, legal, healthcare, finance, insurance, or any business where errors matter, you don't want bravado from your AI stack. You want disciplined behavior. The new org chart isn't just about productivity. It's also about governance. Who owns final approval? Which system is the source of truth? Which actions can happen automatically? What must be reviewed? What gets logged? What gets escalated? Who is accountable when something goes wrong?

Those are org-chart questions now. And the companies that win with agents will treat organizational design as an operating discipline, not an administrative exercise.

There's another point here that entrepreneurs need to hear clearly: a hybrid workforce doesn't eliminate management. In some ways, it raises the standard for it.

If you can't clearly define a role, you'll struggle to build an effective agent for it. If you can't articulate what success looks like, you'll struggle to evaluate the output. If you can't separate judgment from repetition, you'll assign the wrong work to the wrong layer. If you can't create clean escalation paths, you'll end up with chaos.

AI doesn't erase weak management. It exposes it.

That's why some founders will get far more out of agents than others. The advantage won't come only from access to models or tools. It'll come from clarity of thought. The founder who can design roles, define standards, and create systems of accountability will have a massive edge over the founder who just piles

AI on top of a messy business.

This is one reason I believe smaller, sharper companies can beat larger incumbents in this transition. Big companies often have more resources, but they also have more organizational inertia—more departments, more politics, more vague ownership, more meetings, more handoffs with no accountability, more people protecting old boxes on the org chart.

A smaller company with a founder who understands hybrid architecture can move much faster. It can redesign roles from the ground up, create specialist agents around actual needs, tighten reporting lines, and use software where software is best, humans where humans are best, and agents where agents are best.

That's not theory. That's a structural advantage.

It also changes what hiring means. In the coming years, one of the smartest questions a founder can ask won't be, "Who do I need to hire next?" but rather, "What capacity does the business need next, and what's the right mix of human, software, and agent to provide it?"

Sometimes the answer will still be a human. Sometimes it should be. If the role depends heavily on judgment, trust, persuasion, relationship nuance, negotiation, leadership, or accountability under uncertainty, a human should remain central. But if the role includes a large percentage of repeatable processing, drafting, routing, monitoring, synthesis, or structured coordination, then an agent probably belongs somewhere in that function.

That doesn't mean replacing the human. It may mean making the human dramatically better. A great closer with agent support can outperform one without it. A strong executive assistant with agent support can operate at a much higher level. A marketing leader with a coordinated set of specialist agents can produce at a pace that used to require a full team. A founder with a well-designed hybrid org chart can run a company that feels larger, sharper, and more responsive than its headcount would suggest.

And I believe we're still early.

Most companies haven't redesigned anything yet. They're still treating AI as an add-on, not as a structural component of the organization—using it for isolated tasks while leaving the architecture untouched. That's fine for experimentation. It's not enough for transformation.

The companies that move first will start to look different internally before they look different externally. Their org charts will quietly change. Their teams will operate differently. Their speed will improve. Their leaders will spend less time in low-value coordination and more time on judgment, relationships, and direction.

From the outside, it may not be obvious at first why they're pulling away. From the inside, the reason will be clear: they redesigned the company around the work, and they stopped assuming that every box on the org chart had to contain a person.

The org chart of the future isn't anti-human. It's pro-clarity. It respects human judgment enough not to waste it. It respects systems enough to define them. It respects specialization enough to design for it. And it respects reality enough to admit that the best businesses from here forward will be hybrid by design.

That's where I believe this goes for almost every legacy business. Not to a fantasy where humans vanish, but to a more capable model where humans lead, software records, agents execute in narrowly defined roles, and the business becomes stronger because the architecture finally matches the work.

Once you see your company that way, you can't unsee it. You stop looking at a team as just a payroll list and start looking at it as a coordinated system. That's when the real redesign begins.

The next question isn't what tool to buy. It's where to begin. Not with toys. Not with demos. Not with whatever AI app showed up in your feed this week.

You begin with the work itself.

Chapter 6

Start With Workflows, Not Toys

I learned this lesson long before AI entered the conversation.

Years ago, building businesses that depended heavily on people, I made a shift that changed everything. I stopped thinking in terms of people first and started thinking in terms of roles first.

That sounds obvious until you actually do it.

Most small and mid-sized businesses aren't really designed. They're accumulated. One good person joins, proves capable, and gradually takes on more. Another comes in and fills gaps that were never clearly defined. Before long, you have people doing jobs that were never written down, never segmented, and never measured. You don't have an operating system. You have a patchwork quilt held together by goodwill, tribal knowledge, and whoever answers Slack messages the fastest.

That works for a while. It doesn't scale.

When I began breaking businesses down by role instead of by person, I could finally see what was actually happening. One person called an administrative assistant might be handling inbox triage, customer communication, data entry, scheduling, status follow-up, and exception handling. A bookkeeper might also be doing vendor management, reporting cleanup, and random operations support. A customer service rep might also be doing retention, upsell recovery, and internal routing.

Most people were wearing multiple hats.

That insight was a game changer. Once I could see the hats, I could evaluate them separately. What does this role actually require? Where are the bottlenecks? Which parts require judgment? Which parts require consistency? Which parts create revenue? Which parts create drag?

That way of thinking matters even more now — because when you move into an agent-powered business, you can't start with the toys. You have to start with the work.

That's where I see so many business owners get distracted.

They get excited about the latest model, the newest app, the coolest interface, the demo that looks like magic, the chatbot with the sexy voice, the image generator, the browser agent, the AI note taker, the workflow builder. They start buying subscriptions. They start playing. They start testing random tools because each one seems to offer a shortcut.

That's not a strategy. That's digital window shopping.

I'm not against the tools. I use them every day. I build with them. I experiment aggressively. I'm early on purpose. But the businesses that will win with AI aren't the ones with the biggest pile of tools. They're the ones that understand their workflows well enough to know exactly where intelligence, automation, routing, and oversight belong.

The real question isn't, "What AI app should I try?"

The real question is, "What work in my business should be redesigned?"

If you miss that, you end up doing what most people are doing right now. You bolt AI onto the edges of your business. You use it to write social media posts. You use it to summarize meetings. You clean up emails. You get a little lift, maybe even a meaningful one, but the underlying operating model stays exactly the same.

You haven't changed the business. You've accessorized it.

I've seen this movie before. In the early internet era, a lot of business owners treated the web like a brochure — same thinking, same assumptions, same business model, different surface. The people who won understood that the medium wasn't the point. The business model change was the point.

AI is the same. Start by asking what shiny thing you can add, and you stay in novelty mode. Start by asking what workflows should be re-architected, and you move into structural advantage.

* * *

A workflow is simply a sequence of work that moves something from one state to another.

Lead to appointment. Order to fulfillment. Inquiry to proposal. File opened to file closed. Invoice received to invoice paid. Content idea to published asset.

Every business is really just a collection of workflows. Some create revenue. Some protect quality. Some reduce risk. Some exist only because the business has grown messy and nobody has bothered to redesign them. That last category is bigger than most people think.

The reason workflows matter so much in an agent-powered business is simple: agents are only useful when they're connected to defined work. Not vague intentions. Not generic tasks. Defined work.

Here's where another important shift happens.

When I used to break a company down into roles, that alone created clarity. But when you begin designing with AI agents, even the role itself is often too large.

In a traditional business, one capable human can handle five different functions because humans are flexible. A strong operator can switch context, improvise, remember exceptions, smooth over ambiguity, and compensate for broken systems. That messiness is part of their power.

Agents are different.

Yes, they can reason. Yes, they can perform a surprising range of work. But if you want an agentic system to be reliable, scalable, and governable, you need to get more specific, not less.

Let me put that plainly.

If you have a person in your company handling "order setup," that sounds like one role. It isn't.

Order intake might involve receiving the request, checking completeness, validating required fields, identifying missing information, determining type, entering data into the system, generating confirmations, routing to the next internal owner, creating follow-up reminders, and escalating exceptions.

That's not one thing. That's a bundle.

A human can carry that bundle. An agent-powered system usually shouldn't.

Instead, you might separate that one "role" into several smaller specialized functions. One agent checks intake completeness. Another classifies the order type. Another prepares structured data for system entry. Another drafts the confirmation. Another monitors for missing items after a set period. Another flags anything that falls outside normal rules.

Now you're thinking correctly.

You're not trying to create one magic robot employee that vaguely behaves like your best operations person. You're designing a workflow. That's a much better way to build — and a much better way to scale.

A specialized agent can often be reused across more than one workflow. A classification agent may support intake, customer service routing, and reporting cleanup. A follow-up agent may support collections, sales nurture, and operations reminders. A document-checking agent may support onboarding, compliance, and fulfillment. Once you start designing at that level, you stop thinking in terms of one-to-one replacement and start thinking in terms of modular capability.

That's how a digital workforce begins to compound.

Some people imagine a business with three agents or five agents, or one super-agent that does everything. That's legacy thinking. If needed, you could have fifty agents. You could have a hundred. The number isn't the issue. The issue is whether they're specialized, governed, documented, and connected to real business outcomes.

Nobody asks how many formulas are in a spreadsheet if the spreadsheet works. Nobody asks how many lines of code are in a software product if the product performs. Over time, nobody will care how many agents are in your business. They'll care whether your business is faster, more accurate, more responsive, more scalable, and more profitable.

That's the scoreboard.

* * *

So where do you start?

Not with a model comparison chart. Not with a prompt library. Not with a list of trending AI tools on X.

Start by identifying the workflows that matter most. I like to look at them through four lenses.

Frequency. How often does this workflow happen? High-frequency work is often where your first gains live, because small improvements repeat. If something occurs ten times a day and it's even moderately inefficient, that drag compounds fast.

Friction. Where does the workflow get stuck, delayed, dropped, reworked, or escalated? Where are your people chasing missing information, answering the same question repeatedly, copying data from one place to another? Friction is where money leaks.

Consequence. Which workflows, when handled badly, create outsized damage? Lost leads. Delayed closings. Billing mistakes. Bad customer experiences. Compliance exposure. A workflow doesn't have to be frequent to matter. A low-frequency, high-consequence workflow can be worth redesigning early.

Repeatability. Can the workflow be broken into clear steps, decision points, and escalation paths? If yes, that's promising. If the work is still entirely undefined, emotional, or dependent on senior-level judgment, it may not be the right first target.

Notice what's missing from those four lenses.

Technology.

That's deliberate. You don't begin with the tool. You begin with the work. Once you understand the work, you can ask what combination of software, automation, AI assistance, specialized agents, and human oversight fits best.

Sometimes the right answer isn't an agent at all. Sometimes a workflow is broken because of bad forms, bad handoffs, or bad ownership. Sometimes a simple automation is enough. Sometimes a dashboard solves the problem. Don't force an agent into a workflow just because you want to feel modern. That's another version of playing with toys.

* * *

The businesses that get the highest return from AI are usually the ones that become more disciplined, not less.

When you map a workflow honestly, you're forced to confront realities that are easy to ignore when humans are compensating for them. You discover nobody has defined what "complete" means for intake. You discover six versions of the same customer communication floating around. You discover exceptions aren't rare at all — the upstream process is broken. You discover three people are touching the same task because nobody trusts the system. You discover your best employee is buried in invisible cleanup work.

That's valuable.

AI doesn't just create the possibility of automation. It exposes operational truth.

That's why workflow mapping is one of the most important strategic exercises a business owner can do right now, even before deploying agents at scale. You can't redesign what you refuse to see. And you definitely can't delegate work to AI when you don't actually understand the work yourself.

Many entrepreneurs know revenue. They know sales. They know product. They know customers. But they don't really know the internal workflows of their own business at a granular level. They know them loosely. They know who to ask. They know who usually handles things.

That's not the same as knowing the workflow.

The companies that pull away over the next few years won't just be the ones with access to better AI. They'll be the ones with better clarity — clearer roles, clearer handoffs, clearer rules, clearer escalation paths, clearer definitions of done. That clarity becomes machine-readable. It becomes automatable. It becomes scalable.

Messiness, by contrast, becomes expensive.

* * *

If you want a practical place to begin, take one workflow and lay it out in plain English from start to finish. Not the ideal version. The real version.

Who starts it? What triggers it? What information is needed? What system is touched? What usually goes wrong? Which decisions are rules-based? Which require judgment? What happens when something is missing? Who gets notified? What does success look like? How long should it take? How often is it late? How often is it done twice?

That exercise alone will teach you a lot.

Then do something even more useful. Break that workflow into micro-functions.

This is the part that translates directly into agent design.

Instead of saying, "We need an AI customer service agent," ask: Do we need an agent that classifies inbound requests? An agent that drafts first-response messages based on context and policy? An agent that checks whether the answer already exists in the knowledge base? An agent that identifies urgency and routes accordingly? An agent that follows up after forty-eight hours if the issue remains unresolved? An agent that summarizes the thread for a human escalation owner?

That's a workflow mindset.

Compare that with how most people approach AI: "I want an AI customer service rep." That sounds efficient. It's actually vague. Vague is where failures hide. Vague is where people start blaming AI for doing exactly what they failed to define.

The tighter and more clearly bounded the agent role is, the easier it is to trust, improve, and redeploy.

Narrow is testable. Narrow is measurable. Narrow is easier to govern, easier to replace if you designed it poorly, and easier for your human team to understand where the agent ends and the human takes over.

That last point matters more than most founders realize. One reason AI projects stall inside companies isn't technical failure — it's role confusion. The human team doesn't know what the AI is supposed to own. The AI is given fuzzy instructions. Nobody knows what good looks like. One weird edge case happens, trust drops, and the whole initiative gets labeled "not ready."

The answer isn't to retreat. The answer is to tighten the workflow.

* * *

If I were sitting with an entrepreneur and had to guide them through this in one afternoon, I'd tell them to create three lists.

List one: workflows that happen constantly. List two: workflows that create the most friction or annoyance for the team. List three: workflows where mistakes are expensive.

Anywhere those lists overlap, you probably have your best starting points.

Then I'd ask a harder question: which parts of those workflows are truly human?

Not because humans are doing them now. Because they should remain human.

There are parts of business that should stay with people because they require trust, discretion, nuanced judgment, persuasion, empathy, or authority. There are other parts being handled by people simply because nobody has redesigned the process yet. Don't confuse those two categories.

A lot of businesses are paying human beings to perform work that should have been turned into system work years ago. That's not respectful of human talent. It's lazy design.

When I say the future is human-led and agent-powered, I don't mean humans get pushed out of meaningful work. I mean humans get pulled upward into more meaningful work. That only happens if you're willing to strip away the low-level repetition, routing, drafting, monitoring, and administrative sprawl that's been sitting on top of them for years.

Workflow design is how you do that.

* * *

Please don't try to redesign everything at once. That's another trap. Founders see the potential, get excited, and try to agentize the entire company in one sweep. Complexity explodes, people get confused, governance breaks down, momentum dies.

You don't need a revolution in one weekend. You need a sequence of wins.

Pick a workflow. Map it honestly. Break it into functions. Decide which functions belong to software, which belong to agents, and which belong to humans. Define the rules. Define the escalation path. Define the finish line. Then test. Then improve. Then stack the next one.

That's how a real system gets built. Not with a demo. With architecture.

The irony is that once you start doing this, the tools become more useful. A powerful model in a sloppy workflow is mostly wasted. A decent model in a well-designed workflow creates immediate value. Stop obsessing over whether one model is 8 percent better than another and start obsessing over whether the workflow is actually defined.

Most of the advantage won't come from the model delta. It will come from the design delta. And because each improvement strengthens other workflows — better classification improves routing everywhere, better exception handling improves escalation system-wide — the compounding effect is real.

That's how an agent-powered business starts to feel different from a traditional one. Not because it has more technology. Because it has more intentionality.

I don't care whether you run a title company, a law firm, an accounting practice, a brokerage, a medical office, a coaching business, a consulting firm, or something else entirely. The pattern is the same. You're already running workflows. Some are clean. Some are wasteful. Some are fragile. Some are invisible until something breaks.

Your job now is to surface them, understand them, and redesign them deliberately.

Not with a chatbot on your homepage. Not with a flashy demo. Not with a random subscription stack.

With the work. Always with the work.

Do this well, and something important shifts. You stop seeing AI as entertainment or novelty or productivity support. You start seeing it as operating infrastructure.

That's the shift. And once you see it that way, you're ready for the next step:

not just mapping workflows, but actually deploying your first autonomous role inside the business — with clarity, boundaries, and accountability.

That's where this gets real.

Chapter 7

The Compounding Business

I learned this lesson long before AI.

When I was building one of my early businesses, growth looked exciting from the outside and exhausting from the inside. Revenue went up, customers came in, opportunities multiplied, and for a while that felt like momentum. But under the hood, every bit of growth demanded another person, another phone line, another layer of management, another training cycle, another point of failure.

That is how most businesses scale.

They don't really scale. They accumulate weight.

You add one more employee to handle the work created by the last employee. Then another manager to supervise the growing group. Then another software subscription to hold everything together. Then you discover the new bottleneck isn't demand — it's coordination.

I saw this in service businesses, real estate, and title. I saw it in the internet era too, but with one major difference: the businesses that won on the internet didn't just add people. They built systems that kept getting more valuable every time a new customer, feature, or process was added.

That's the shift most people still don't understand about agent-powered companies.

Humans scale linearly.

Well-built agent systems don't.

That doesn't mean humans become irrelevant. It means the economics change. A strong human operator can do more. A small team can behave like a much larger one. A founder can build capability without rebuilding the payroll every time the company wants to grow.

That's what makes this moment important.

Most entrepreneurs still think AI is about making one task faster. Write an email. Summarize a meeting. Draft a social post. That's useful, but it's small thinking. It's productivity thinking.

What I care about is compounding.

Compounding is when the second improvement makes the first improvement more valuable. The third agent makes the first two better. Every workflow you map, every rule you define, every exception you document, every memory you preserve, and every system you connect starts increasing the value of everything around it.

That's not a tool. That's a business model advantage.

I've spent enough years building companies to know the pain of linear scaling. In my short sale business, we had 18 processors, an in-house title team, marketing reps, and a highly structured operation. For that time, it was advanced. We were paperless earlier than most. We had process, documentation, specialization. And still, growth had a ceiling because every increase in volume created more operational load. More files meant more people. More people meant more training. More training meant more inconsistency. More inconsistency meant more management attention.

That's not failure. That's the math of labor-heavy business.

The same dynamic plays out in brokerages, law firms, title companies, agencies, medical practices, accounting firms, and home service businesses. The founder tells himself he wants scale. What he actually has is a bigger version of the same machine with more payroll and more stress.

The internet changed that equation for certain kinds of businesses — it allowed distribution and delivery to separate from geography and labor in ways most people had never seen before. The businesses that mattered didn't just use the internet to communicate. They rebuilt around what the internet made possible. The early movers weren't always the biggest. They were the ones learning faster than everyone else while the rest of the market debated whether the opportunity was real.

That's exactly where we are now with AI agents.

If you build around the old model and sprinkle AI on top, you might get 10 or 15 percent more efficient.

If you redesign around agents, memory, workflows, escalation rules, and human oversight, you can build a company with entirely different economics.

That's the real prize.

A normal business grows by adding labor. A slightly better business grows by adding software. A compounding business grows by building reusable intelligence.

Reusable intelligence is any instruction, decision pattern, workflow, dataset, prompt, escalation rule, or learned context that improves future execution without requiring a human to rediscover it every time.

Once you understand that, you begin to see the opportunity everywhere.

The first time your team handles an exception, you solve a problem. The second time, if the knowledge is captured correctly, you improve the system. The tenth time, if that knowledge is embedded inside an agent-driven workflow, the company is no longer merely reacting. It's accumulating operational intelligence.

That accumulation is where the compounding starts.

A human employee gets better over time. That matters. But the improvement is trapped inside one person unless you extract it, document it, train it, and enforce it across the team. People are inconsistent. They leave. They forget. They improvise. They bring judgment — which is valuable — but they also bring variation, which is expensive.

An agent system can preserve and repeat what works. Not perfectly. Not without guardrails. But once a rule is clarified, once a workflow is mapped, once a quality check is defined, that improvement can be deployed again and again at a cost that's radically different from hiring and retraining another person.

This is why the future belongs to human-led, agent-powered businesses.

The human part remains essential. Humans decide what matters. Humans define acceptable risk. Humans handle trust, judgment, negotiation, ethics, brand, relationships, and final calls. Humans create the vision and determine when the machine is wrong.

But agents can carry a growing share of everything around that core: research, monitoring, drafting, routing, follow-up, reporting, summarization, exception flagging, checklist enforcement, status synchronization, first-pass review.

That's where the economics start to change.

Let me make that concrete. Imagine five agents deployed inside one business.

One monitors inbound requests. One drafts responses. One checks files against a process standard. One updates the CRM. One creates a manager report at the end of the day.

Most people look at those five and think: that saves labor.

Yes, but that's the smallest benefit.

The bigger benefit is what happens between them. The monitoring agent feeds better information to the drafting agent. The drafting agent creates more standardized communication for the CRM agent to categorize. The CRM agent improves the manager report. The process-check agent identifies recurring exceptions, which informs future workflow design.

The system isn't just doing tasks. It's making itself more visible.

Visibility compounds. Standardization compounds. Speed compounds. Data compounds.

This is where early movers begin building advantages that late movers struggle to see, let alone match.

Most companies ask, "How can we save time?"

The better question is: "How can we build a business that gets more capable every month without growing complexity at the same rate?"

That's the compounding business.

And let me be direct: this is not a theory exercise for me.

At Cloud Title, we're not pretending we've solved this. We're in the middle of building. We use Qualia as the core production platform. We've adopted Qualia Clear. We're building workflow automations outside that environment. An automated transaction coordinator, municipal lien search automation, a real estate assistant, frameworks that connect operating data to follow-up and marketing systems.

Some of it is working. Some is early. Some is messy.

The point isn't that the transformation is complete. The point is that once you start building the right way, you can feel the economics shift. A workflow that used to depend on one busy person becomes a partially structured system. A report that required manual effort becomes repeatable. A recurring exception becomes a candidate for automation instead of a permanent annoyance.

That's how a company begins to compound. Not through magic. Through accumulation.

I'm doing the same thing with OpenClaw in a different context. OpenClaw isn't a finished product. It's a live operating environment — multiple agents handling specialized roles across strategy, operations, content, research, and engineering functions. What matters to me isn't the novelty of having multiple agents. It's what happens when the system starts retaining context, improving coordination, and reducing the amount of founder energy required to move work forward.

That's the deeper value.

When founders first experiment with agents, they usually think in terms of substitution. Can this replace an assistant? A coordinator? Part of a marketer's role? Sometimes that's the right question. Usually it's not the most important one.

The more important question is: what new capacity does this create once it becomes part of a connected system?

A single agent that drafts meeting summaries is useful. A connected set of agents that summarize meetings, extract next steps, assign owners, update project memory, generate follow-up communication, and surface unresolved blockers to the right human is something else entirely. That second model doesn't merely save time. It changes execution speed.

Execution speed, over time, isn't a small advantage. It's a structural one.

If one company can turn decisions into action in two days and another takes two weeks, the faster company doesn't just move first — it learns first. And if one company documents and preserves what it learns while the other keeps rediscovering the same operational mistakes, the gap widens further.

That widening is what most incumbents misread. They think the early mover's advantage comes from novelty. It usually comes from iteration speed.

By the time the laggards decided the internet mattered, the leaders had already built distribution, customer habits, process knowledge, vendor relationships, brand trust, and technical infrastructure. The window didn't stay open for very long.

It never does.

This is also why small and mid-sized companies have a real opening here. In the past, major operational advantages required major capital — big software projects, large implementation teams, dedicated IT departments, enterprise budgets. Now, a sharp founder with the right mindset can begin building a real agentic operating layer inside a relatively small company. Not overnight, not without mistakes, but without waiting for a board meeting, a national rollout, or a seven-figure transformation budget.

A disciplined entrepreneur can now build capability that used to belong only to bigger players. That's a massive change.

Because AI, used correctly, changes the relationship between scale and headcount. It changes the relationship between complexity and control. It changes the relationship between founder ambition and operational drag.

For years, one of the cruel realities of entrepreneurship was that growth often made life worse before it made life better. More customers created more chaos. More revenue created more payroll pressure. The founder became the glue holding an increasingly complex machine together.

A compounding business breaks that pattern — not fully at first, but directionally and unmistakably.

Each well-designed agent reduces friction in one place and creates information that improves another. Each documented workflow becomes easier to delegate to a machine and easier for a human to supervise. Each preserved decision pattern lowers the cost of future execution.

Over time, the company stops behaving like a labor pile and starts behaving like a system.

A labor pile can make money. A system can build enterprise value. Those are not the same thing.

If your business depends on hardworking people constantly pushing work uphill, you may have a good business, but you also have a fragile one. If your business is increasingly defined by reusable workflows, preserved operating intelligence, agent-supported execution, and human judgment placed exactly where it matters most, you're building something much harder to displace.

Early movers in this cycle aren't just getting efficient. They're building moats.

Not the kind that came from patents, capital, or geography. A new kind. Workflow moats. Memory moats. Speed moats. Decision moats. Data moats.

And because these moats are operational rather than promotional, they're difficult to copy from the outside. A competitor can copy your website, your offer, your marketing language. He can't easily copy the operating system underneath your company if it's been built, refined, connected, and improved over time.

That's why timing matters.

The first few agents aren't the finish line. They're the beginning of the compounding curve.

At first, the results feel modest. A little faster. A little cleaner. A little less manual. A little more visible. Then the curve starts bending. The business has memory. It has repeatable patterns. It has execution support that doesn't disappear at 5 p.m. The founder is no longer trying to personally carry every gap.

This is when the business starts becoming more than the sum of its people.

That doesn't diminish people. It frees them. Your best people work at the level they were meant to work. Managers handle exceptions instead of drowning in routine. Specialists focus on judgment instead of status chasing. The founder designs the future instead of playing permanent catch-up with the present.

That's the real promise of the compounding business. Not fewer humans. Better use of them.

And once you see that clearly, the next question is obvious.

If the real opportunity isn't casual AI usage, and isn't even workflow mapping alone, but the deployment of a true role-based agent inside your business — where do you begin?

That's where we go next.

Because at some point, theory has to become a hire. Not a human hire. Your first autonomous one.

Part III:
The Build

Chapter 8

Your First Autonomous Hire

The first time most business owners say they want an AI employee, what they really mean is this: they're tired.

Tired of following up. Tired of checking whether something was done. Tired of work that's important but not worthy of their attention. Tired of paying good people to do low-value coordination work because there's never been another option.

They don't need another demo. They don't need a chatbot that writes a clever paragraph.

They need help.

Real help. The kind that wakes up, knows its job, touches the right systems, produces a result, and escalates when it reaches the edge of its authority.

That's the standard. If you don't start there, you'll end up where a lot of companies are right now: impressed by AI in the abstract and unchanged in the real world.

I want this chapter to be concrete, because this is where the conversation stops being intellectual. We've talked about why the shift matters, why the org chart changes, why workflows matter, and why the economics of an agent-powered business are different. Now we move from theory into build.

Your first autonomous hire is not a chatbot. It's not a prompt you paste into

ChatGPT once in a while. It's not a novelty hanging off the side of your company. It's a role.

A seat. A lane. A job that exists because the business needs it to exist.

Years ago, one of the biggest breakthroughs I made in traditional business came when I stopped thinking in terms of people and started thinking in terms of roles. In small businesses especially, one strong person often carries five jobs. She answers the phone, handles customer service, follows up on documents, fixes mistakes, and remembers what nobody else remembered. Then the owner says, "She's amazing." Of course she is — she's doing the work of an entire mini-department.

But that model hides the truth. You don't have a talent problem. You have a series of functions that need to be defined, separated, measured, and improved.

The same logic applies here.

If you want to make your first autonomous hire successfully, don't begin by asking, "What can AI do?" Ask instead: "What role needs to exist in my business, and what portion of that role can be reliably handled by an agent?"

That question is better. It's practical. It forces specificity. It prevents fantasy. And it protects you from one of the biggest mistakes founders make in this phase: trying to hire AI for a job they haven't even defined properly for a human.

If the role is fuzzy, the agent will be fuzzy. If the instructions are vague, the output will be vague. If you can't define success, the agent can't produce it.

You don't hire your first autonomous agent by starting with the smartest model. You hire it by starting with the clearest job.

—

When I say "autonomous," I don't mean unsupervised and unchecked. I mean the agent can execute within a defined scope without needing to be manually prompted every single time. It has triggers. It has responsibilities. It has boundaries. It has an output. It has an owner. It has a scorecard.

That's what makes it a hire rather than a toy.

Here's a distinction worth making.

A prompt is a request. A workflow is a sequence. An autonomous hire is an operating role inside your company.

If I ask AI to summarize meeting notes, that's a task. If I build a workflow that transcribes meetings, extracts action items, sends a summary, and archives the notes, that's a process. If I assign an agent responsibility for meeting intelligence across the company — capturing notes, surfacing action items, detecting missed follow-up, escalating unresolved items to the right human owner — that's a role.

Most businesses are still playing at the task level. A few are reaching workflow level. The companies that pull ahead are going to build at the role level — where you stop using AI occasionally and start redesigning how the company actually operates.

—

So what should your first autonomous hire be?

Not your closer. Not your head of strategy. Not your bookkeeper with authority to move money. And not some grand all-purpose "AI assistant" that's supposed to do a little bit of everything — that's almost always a mistake.

Your first autonomous hire should sit in the middle of four conditions: the work happens frequently; the work follows a recognizable pattern; the work creates pain when it's missed; and the downside of partial failure is manageable.

That last one matters more than people think. You don't learn autonomy by handing the keys to the vault to a brand-new digital employee. You learn it by handing over a meaningful but controlled responsibility and watching whether the agent can carry it consistently.

Think in terms of burden, not glamour. The best first role is rarely glamorous. It's usually something like intake, triage, monitoring, research assembly, follow-up coordination, status reporting, exception spotting, or draft generation with human review.

Founders resist this because they want the big win — the AI closer, the AI strategist, the AI rainmaker. I understand the impulse. It's also backwards.

Your first autonomous hire isn't about replacing your highest-level judgment. It's about creating trust in the system. Trust is earned operationally. The first agent has one job beyond the work itself: prove that autonomy can be designed, managed, and measured inside your company.

I'd rather see a founder deploy an agent that reliably monitors open tasks, flags missing documents, drafts follow-up messages, and routes issues correctly than brag about an "AI COO" that mostly produces clever language and confusion.

A real business is built on reliability. So is an agent-powered business.

—

Here's the framework I'd use to choose the first role.

Find a job that's repetitive enough to define, important enough to matter, bounded enough to control, and annoying enough that your team will immediately feel the relief when it works. You're looking for the role where the business says, "Thank God that's handled" — not, "That was an interesting experiment."

Once you identify it, write the job description. Literally.

Don't skip this. Write it as if you were hiring a human. What's the mission of the role? What systems does it touch? What triggers the work? What exactly is it supposed to do? What decisions can it make on its own, and which require escalation? What does "done" look like? How will you measure whether it's working? Who owns it?

If you can't answer those questions on one page, you're not ready to hire the agent.

—

Let me give you a concrete example.

Suppose you run a real estate business and one of the constant breakdowns is lead follow-up. People fill out forms. Someone on the team means to respond. Some leads are called quickly. Some get a text. Some sit. Some are forgotten until it's too late. Then everybody says the leads are bad.

Maybe the leads are bad. But often the system is worse.

Your first autonomous hire in that environment might be an inquiry response coordinator. Its mission isn't "do sales." Its mission is narrower and more useful: monitor inbound inquiries, categorize them by source and intent, draft the first response based on the right template and context, log the lead in the CRM correctly, assign it to the right human owner, and surface any inquiry that hasn't received human contact within a defined time window.

That's a real role. It has a lane. It creates immediate operational benefit. It doesn't require the agent to persuade, negotiate, or promise things it shouldn't promise. And it creates measurable outputs: response time, routing accuracy, completion rate, leads without contact. You can manage that.

Here's another example from a title or transaction environment. A strong first autonomous hire might be an exception monitor. Its mission: inspect files at defined intervals, compare actual file status against expected milestones, detect missing items, summarize the exception, and notify the assigned human with a recommended next action.

Notice what the agent isn't doing. It's not approving wire transfers. It's not giving legal advice. It's not making final underwriting decisions. It's doing something extremely valuable: persistent, disciplined oversight of work that humans do poorly when the day gets busy.

This is where the ROI hides — in the gap between "important" and "boring."

—

Once the role is selected and the job description is written, the build begins. Here's how I break it down.

Define the role in one sentence. If you need a paragraph, it's too broad. Example: "The agent monitors incoming customer inquiries, drafts the appropriate first response, logs the interaction correctly, and escalates any ambiguity or urgency to the assigned team member." That's clear.

Define the inputs. What information can the agent see — email inbox, CRM records, forms, project management tasks, internal SOPs, templates? A lot of agent projects fail right here because the founder is excited about autonomy but hasn't thought through access. You can't expect an agent to operate intelligently if it's blind, fragmented, or pulling from five conflicting sources of truth. Small businesses actually have an advantage: you can simplify faster. Decide that for this role, three systems matter. Everything else is out of scope. That discipline wins.

Define the actions — verb by verb. Don't say "help manage leads." Say: reads inbound inquiries, classifies inquiry type, checks contact record, selects the correct message template, drafts a personalized response, creates or updates the CRM record, assigns the owner, and flags inquiries with missing information. Now we're building something.

Define the authority boundary. Can it send the first reply automatically, or only draft it? Can it update the CRM directly, or only recommend changes? Can it assign tasks, or only suggest owners? This isn't a philosophical question — it's a risk-management question. Your first autonomous hire should have a narrow authority boundary. That doesn't make it weak; it makes it safe. I'd rather run an agent in a tightly bounded lane at 90 percent reliability than give it broad authority at 40 percent reliability and then conclude that "AI isn't ready." The architecture wasn't ready.

Define escalation — and don't skip this. A good human employee knows when to raise a hand. A good AI agent must be designed to do the same. What should trigger escalation? Ambiguity. Missing critical information. A customer complaint. A compliance-sensitive issue. A conflict between data sources. A deadline risk. A low-confidence interpretation. Don't wait for the agent to figure out when it should escalate. Tell it. Spell it out. Give examples. Make the edge visible.

Define the output. Where does the work show up — in a dashboard, in Slack, in the CRM, in a daily report? You want visible work, not hidden work. A lot of founders are seduced by the idea of a silent machine doing magic in the background. I prefer visibility, especially early. If the agent handled twenty-five items today, I want to see the twenty-five. If it escalated three, I want to see why. Opacity is the enemy of trust.

Assign a scorecard. If the agent is a hire, it gets measured. Keep it simple: accuracy, completion rate, cycle time, escalation rate, rework required, human overrides. The point isn't a giant KPI framework on day one — it's making the role accountable to outcomes rather than vibes. If you can't tell whether the agent is doing a good job, the system will drift into storytelling. One person says it's amazing. Another says it's making mistakes. A third says it saved time but nobody knows how much. Measure it. You'd do that with a real hire.

—

Now, what not to do.

Don't start with a role that exists mostly in your imagination. Don't start with a role that requires broad business judgment before you've proven narrower execution. Don't give the first agent six disconnected jobs just because you're excited. Don't let ten team members give it different instructions.

And don't skip ownership. Every agent needs a manager — not metaphorically, literally. Who reviews the scorecard? Who updates the instructions? Who checks failure patterns? Who tightens the SOP? Who decides whether the authority boundary expands?

If nobody owns the agent, it becomes orphaned technology. And orphaned technology is everywhere. That's why so many software stacks grow while businesses don't. Tools without ownership don't compound. They clutter.

—

Before you turn anything loose in production, run a shadow phase.

Let the agent perform the job in parallel first. Have it read the inputs, produce the outputs, make the recommendations — but don't let it fully execute yet. Compare its work against what a strong human operator would have done. Where did it interpret correctly? Where did it miss nuance? Where did it escalate appropriately? Where did it act too confidently?

This is where you earn the right to expand authority. You don't jump from zero to full autonomy. You graduate into it.

The progression I like: first the agent observes, then it drafts, then it recommends, then it executes within a narrow lane, then it earns broader responsibility. That sounds slower than founders want. It's usually faster than cleaning up after a rushed rollout. The companies that do this well aren't always the ones with the best models. They're the ones with the best discipline.

That discipline matters even more when the agent touches customers. If your first agent has any external-facing responsibility, your brand is on the line. Tone matters. Timing matters. Context matters. You can't hide behind "the AI did it" — the customer still experiences your company.

Good first external-facing roles: first-response drafts, appointment coordination, FAQ handling inside clear policy limits, status updates, reminders. Bad examples: free-form negotiation, complaint resolution without human visibility, anything that requires making commitments the company may have to honor later.

—

There's a benefit here that people often miss.

Your first autonomous hire shouldn't just save labor. It should improve consistency — and that's often more valuable.

A human team can sometimes absorb more work by pushing harder for a season. What breaks them is inconsistency. Some things get done beautifully. Some get missed. Some depend entirely on who remembered what.

An agent, properly designed, starts flattening that inconsistency. It doesn't get tired at 4:30 p.m. It doesn't forget to check the queue because the day got emotional. It doesn't avoid a repetitive task because it's boring. That consistency raises the floor of the company. And once the floor rises, growth gets easier.

This is one reason I believe the entrepreneurs who figure this out early are going to look unnaturally fast compared with their competitors. Not just lower labor intensity — their systems keep moving while other companies are still depending on memory, heroics, and manual follow-up.

—

A reality check from my own world.

At Cloud Title and across the broader systems I'm building, I'm deeply invested in agentic workflows, digital workers, orchestration, and autonomous operating models. But I'm careful not to confuse "building toward" with "already solved." We're in the build. We're testing, refining, learning, tightening. That honesty matters. It's easy to talk big in AI right now. It's more useful to build something real and let the credibility come from the work.

That's exactly the mindset to bring to your first autonomous hire. Don't oversell it. Don't pretend it's magic. Don't call it transformation just because it sent three emails. Build a real role. Give it a real job. Measure the result. Then expand from proof.

—

Here's the simplest way to know whether you chose the right first role.

Within thirty days, a strong operator on your team should say some version of this: "This is actually useful. I want more of this." Not because it's flashy. Because it removed friction. Because it made the team faster. Because it created breathing room.

There's another good signal: when the agent starts revealing process flaws you didn't fully appreciate before. Once you define the role tightly enough for an agent to do it, you suddenly discover the underlying process was never as clear as people thought. The data is messy. The source of truth is inconsistent. The handoff rules are fuzzy. That's not a failure of the agent — that's the agent exposing operational truth. Use it.

One of the hidden benefits of building autonomous roles is that it forces management maturity. You can't hide behind tribal knowledge anymore. You can't keep saying, "Sarah just knows how to do it." You have to define what "it" is. That discipline improves the human side of your company too.

—

One more thing I want to say directly.

Don't frame this internally as "we're replacing people with AI" unless your goal is fear, resistance, and sabotage. The better frame: we're redesigning the company so humans spend more time where judgment, trust, and relationships matter, and less time babysitting repetition.

That's both more accurate and more useful. Some roles will shrink. Some jobs will change. Some tasks will disappear — we should be honest about that. But if you're building this correctly, the first autonomous hire shouldn't create panic. It should create relief.

The team should feel the difference between being burdened by noise and being supported by systems. That's a leadership challenge as much as a technical one.

—

By now you may have noticed I've said almost nothing about model selection, temperature settings, or technical architecture. Intentional.

Those things matter. But most companies don't fail because they chose the wrong model. They fail because they chose the wrong role, set the wrong boundaries, ignored ownership, skipped measurement, and confused capability with readiness.

Founders love talking tools. Operators win with design.

Your first autonomous hire isn't a technology decision. It's an operating decision. You're deciding that a specific role in your company deserves to exist in a more scalable form. You're defining the mission, the lane, the authority, the escalation path, and the scorecard. Then you're earning trust one cycle at a time.

Not with hype. Not with screenshots. With work.

——

If I were advising a founder tomorrow, I'd tell them to do four things this week.

Identify one recurring burden in the company — frequent, patterned, painful, controllable. Write the one-page job description for the autonomous version of that role. Define what the agent can do, what it can't do, and when it must escalate. Run it in shadow mode long enough to compare its work against a strong human operator.

Do that, and you'll know more than most people talking about AI online. More important, you'll have started building the muscle that matters.

Because the first autonomous hire isn't the end of the story. It's the moment your company begins to learn how to manage digital workers as part of the business itself.

Once you have one role working, the next questions arrive fast. What should it remember? What should it forget? What rules govern it? What happens when it fails, drifts, or reaches a trust boundary?

That's where this gets serious. And that's where we go next.

Chapter 9

Memory, Governance, and Trust

O ne of the strangest moments in this whole journey was not some dramatic AI breakthrough. It was a stupid message.

Not once. Over and over.

A reboot notice. Then another. Then another. Followed by chatter that should not have existed in the first place.

Nothing catastrophic happened. No money disappeared. No client data got exposed. But it annoyed me immediately, because I knew exactly what it meant.

The system was doing what it had been told to do, but not what I actually wanted it to do.

That is where this chapter begins.

Most people are still looking at AI through the lens of output. Can it write the email? Can it summarize the meeting? Can it respond to the customer?

That is the shallow end of the pool.

The real game starts when the system is no longer just generating words, but operating over time. The moment an agent is allowed to persist, remember, trigger, route, and act repeatedly, the conversation changes. Now you are not dealing with a novelty. You are dealing with behavior.

And behavior without memory, governance, and trust is just automation with better grammar.

If you are going to build an agent-powered business, memory is not a nice feature. Governance is not a legal afterthought. Trust is not a branding issue. Those three things are the difference between a serious operating system and a very expensive way to create new kinds of chaos.

That repeated reboot chatter was not a major problem in isolation. But it was a gift, because it exposed a truth that applies to every entrepreneur building with AI: small governance flaws become large credibility problems once systems start running continuously. A duplicated cron job. An agent that remembers the wrong instruction. A workflow acting on stale context. None of these sound dramatic when you describe them. In a live business, they matter.

Because the minute people stop trusting the system, they stop using it. And when they stop using it, the whole promise collapses.

I learned a version of this lesson long before AI. In the early internet days, a lot of businesses wanted the appearance of being online before they had the operational discipline to support it. They wanted the website, the email address, the ecommerce storefront — but they had not thought through uptime, routing, billing, security, or failure recovery. They wanted the shiny front end without the operational backbone.

It never worked for long.

AI is creating the same temptation all over again. People want the agent demo. They want the autonomous workflow. They want the dashboard screenshot. But once you move from toy to system, three questions become unavoidable.

What does this thing remember?

What is it allowed to do?

Why should anyone trust it?

Those are not technical questions. They are business design questions.

Memory is where most founders get seduced and then blindsided.

When people hear the word "memory" in AI, they often imagine the system becoming smarter because it can remember everything forever. That sounds appealing until you realize that remembering everything is often the fastest route to confusion.

Good memory is not about maximum accumulation. It is about useful continuity.

A well-designed agent does not need to remember every sentence ever written. It needs to remember the right things at the right level for the right purpose.

If I have an agent helping with content, it should remember my voice, my positioning, my brand standards. It does not need to remember every random brainstorm I abandoned at midnight. If I have an agent handling customer follow-up, it should remember the status of the relationship, the last meaningful interaction, the next expected step, and any critical constraints. If I have an agent inside a regulated business like title, memory becomes even more sensitive — structured access to file status, milestones, required tasks, approved communication rules. It absolutely does not have permission to freestyle around compliance boundaries.

That is the first principle: memory must be designed, not accumulated.

I think about memory in layers. There is short-term working memory — what the agent needs for the task in front of it. There is role memory — what the agent should know repeatedly because it belongs to the job. And there is business memory — what belongs to the company and not to any single session, model, or experiment.

Founders get into trouble when they mix those layers together.

An agent that carries too little memory becomes useless. You have to repeat yourself every time. It feels like hiring someone with amnesia. An agent that carries too much unmanaged memory becomes unstable — dragging old instructions into new situations, acting on outdated assumptions, creating false confidence because it sounds consistent while being wrong.

I have seen both. The first version frustrates you. The second version can hurt you.

A founder needs to decide what deserves persistence. What belongs in a durable project file. What belongs in a role definition. What belongs in a temporary session. What must be versioned. What must be reviewed by a human. And what should be forgotten on purpose.

That last one matters. Forgetting is not failure. Strategic forgetting is hygiene.

A lot of teams are going to build agent systems that become unreliable simply because nobody made decisions about what the system should stop carrying forward.

If memory answers the question "What does the system know?", governance answers the more important one: "What is the system allowed to do with what it knows?"

This is where the adult work begins.

Governance sounds boring to people who are still drunk on possibility. I get it. It is more fun to talk about what your agents might do than what they should not. But in real business, the limits are where the value is protected.

Governance is how you prevent an agent from becoming a confident intern with admin access.

Every serious agent in a business should have a defined role, a decision boundary, an approval threshold, an escalation path, and an audit trail. Not because we are trying to slow the system down, but because we are trying to make it usable at scale. Without governance, you do not have an operating model. You have a risk surface.

When I think about governance, I start with the human analogy. If I hired a new team member tomorrow, would I just say "use your judgment" and then let them touch clients, finances, scheduling, and systems with no policy, no review standard, and no scope definition? Of course not. Yet that is exactly how many people are deploying AI agents. Broad access, vague goals, no structured boundaries. Then they act surprised when the system behaves inconsistently.

That is not an AI problem. That is a management failure.

In my world — whether I am thinking about OpenClaw, Cloud Title, or any future AI-native business — governance starts with role clarity. Who is this agent? What is its job? What is not its job? What tools can it touch? What data can it access? When must it stop and escalate? What evidence should exist after it acts?

Those questions are not red tape. They are architecture.

An agent summarizing meeting notes can have fairly broad latitude. An agent drafting a client-facing message should operate inside approved brand

and compliance rules. An agent scheduling appointments needs to know exactly what conflicts require escalation. An agent operating anywhere near money movement, legal exposure, or regulated communications should be under much tighter constraints.

This is one reason I believe so strongly in hybrid workforce design. Humans are not disappearing from the system. Humans become the governance layer. They define authority. They approve exceptions. They review edge cases. They own the ethical and commercial consequences. Agents increase capability. Humans remain accountable.

That is not a temporary compromise. I believe it is the right architecture.

A lot of people think trust in AI means accuracy. Accuracy matters, obviously. But trust is bigger.

Trust means predictability. Trust means the system behaves within its lane. Trust means that when it does not know, it does not bluff. Trust means it escalates when it should. Trust means you can inspect what happened afterward. Trust means the people around it know what to expect.

This is why I do not trust agents because they sound smart. I trust agents when they behave reliably.

A smooth sentence is not evidence. An audit trail is evidence. A clean escalation is evidence. Consistency under defined conditions is evidence. Silence when the system should remain silent is evidence.

This is one of the great traps of this era. Language creates the illusion of competence. A traditional software error usually announces itself. Something breaks. A field fails. A button does not work. The issue is visible. An AI agent can fail much more elegantly. It can produce something plausible — sound calm, structured, and helpful — while being wrong in a way that slips past a rushed operator.

Trust has to be earned behaviorally, not emotionally.

When I think about what separates serious builders from people playing around, I keep coming back to a handful of disciplines.

Serious builders define identity before capability. They decide who the agent is supposed to be before they obsess over what model or tool to use. They define memory intentionally — what should persist, where it lives, and who owns it. They create decision boundaries and do not let the system wander into ambiguity without a handoff rule. They build escalation paths so the system knows when to stop. They insist on observability: if the agent acts, there should be a way to inspect what happened. They preserve the human veto — a kill switch is not pessimism, it is professionalism. And they review drift, because a system that was useful six weeks ago can become brittle or misaligned if nobody tends it.

These disciplines are not glamorous. They are exactly why most companies will not build real agentic advantage even though the tools are available to almost everyone. The advantage is not in access to the model. It is in the operating discipline around the model.

Suppose you want to build an AI follow-up system for prospects.

A weak implementation says: "when a lead comes in, have AI respond." That sounds fine until the lead asks an unusual question, or the CRM record is incomplete, or the prospect already spoke with someone on your team, or the system sends a tone-deaf follow-up using stale context from a previous pipeline stage.

A governed implementation is different. It knows the pipeline stage. It knows the last approved contact. It knows which fields are required before any outreach occurs. It knows the approved tone and offer. It knows what objections it can address. It knows what questions require human review. It logs what it sent. It pauses when confidence is low or data is incomplete.

Same category of task. Completely different level of trustworthiness.

Take scheduling. A toy assistant books time. A governed assistant understands availability rules, buffer requirements, priority tiers, travel constraints, who can be double-booked and who cannot, and what kinds of meetings require manual review. The first one saves time until it causes embarrassment. The second one becomes part of the operating fabric.

Or take a regulated business. It is easy to sell the dream of autonomy when there is no real compliance burden. It is much harder when timing, documentation, approvals, accuracy, and auditability actually matter.

Cloud Title is a live proving ground for me, precisely because it is not a toy business. It is a real company in a regulated environment, with real people, real files, real deadlines, and real consequences. We are early in the AI buildout there. The transformation is not complete, and I do not pretend otherwise. But that is exactly why the lessons are credible. In a business like that, you cannot throw an agent into production and hope for the best. You need role design, permissions, exception handling, clean handoffs, and humans who still own judgment. If there is a title issue, a payoff inconsistency, or a communication that touches legal or financial exposure, the system must know where its lane ends. That is not a weakness of AI. That is respect for reality.

I look at agent trust almost the same way I look at human trust. Nobody starts with unlimited authority. You earn range. You earn autonomy. You earn access.

Start with low-risk, high-frequency tasks. Watch the behavior. Review the outputs. Tighten the memory. Clarify the boundaries. Fix the edge cases. Then expand scope. Do not start by asking whether the agent can do everything. Start by asking whether it can do one thing repeatedly, clearly, and safely.

That is how real autonomy gets built. Not in one leap. In layers.

This is also why I am skeptical of founders who talk about replacing people before they have built trustworthy systems. Replacing labor is not the first move. Building governed capability is the first move. Once that capability becomes dependable, the labor model changes naturally. But if you start with the fantasy of instant replacement, you will usually create fear inside the company, overreach in the system, and fragile workflows nobody actually trusts. Then the whole initiative gets labeled a failure when the real problem was reckless sequencing.

The order matters. First clarity. Then control. Then trust. Then scale.

One point that does not get enough attention is ownership. Who owns the memory? Who owns the policy? Who owns the agent's behavior when it goes wrong?

A lot of companies are going to discover that they built "smart" systems with no real ownership structure. Marketing thought sales owned it. Sales thought operations owned it. IT thought somebody else was handling policy. Nobody owned the memory file. Nobody reviewed the prompts. Nobody updated the boundaries when the business changed. That is how drift becomes institutional.

In a serious business, every meaningful agent needs a human owner. Not because the human has to do the work, but because somebody must be responsible for the role definition, the policies, the review cadence, the exception design, and the business outcome. The owner is not there to babysit the system. The owner is there to govern it.

In the coming years, one of the most important management skills in business will be agent governance. Not prompt writing. Not dabbling. Governance. Can you define roles clearly? Can you separate durable memory from temporary context? Can you specify where judgment still belongs to a person? Can you build escalation rules that people actually follow? Can you create a review loop that improves trust instead of slowly eroding it?

That is management in an agent-powered company. And the founders who get good at that are going to build businesses that feel radically more capable than their headcount suggests.

I said earlier that the reboot chatter was a gift. Here is why.

It was a visible, annoying reminder that systems do not become trustworthy by sounding intelligent. They become trustworthy when the architecture is disciplined enough that even small failures are caught, contained, and corrected.

Not perfection. Discipline.

Useful memory. Clear boundaries. Reliable behavior. Human accountability.

Get those pieces right and trust grows. When trust grows, adoption grows. When adoption grows, the business starts to change structurally — because now work is moving through systems that remember the right things, follow the right rules, and know when to hand off to a human being.

That is a very different company. It is also a much more defensible one.

Anyone can get access to a model. Far fewer can build a trusted agent architecture around it.

That is where the moat begins.

The businesses that win in the next decade will not just be the ones with the smartest agents. They will be the ones with the most trustworthy systems.

In the next chapter, I'm going to show you the live laboratory I'm building right now — not the polished fantasy version, but the real one. What we're testing. What's working. What's still messy. Because the theory matters, but the build is where the truth shows up.

Chapter 10

What I'm Building Right Now

I spend a lot of time these days staring at things that don't yet work the way I want them to.

That's not a complaint. It's the job.

On one screen, I've got my title company open. On another, an agent framework, a workflow map, a prompt chain, a failed run, or a report from one of the AI systems I'm building. On another, I'm looking at a bottleneck that's existed in business for twenty years and asking a simple question: why does a human still have to do this by hand?

That question is behind almost everything I'm building right now.

Not because I dislike people. I've built people-heavy companies. I know what it looks like when smart, good people spend their days trapped inside repetitive work, status chasing, manual follow-up, avoidable rework, and a thousand tiny tasks that create activity but not enterprise value. I know what it costs. Money, obviously. But also speed. Consistency. Morale. And eventually, scale.

So when people ask me what I'm building, the cleanest answer is this: I'm trying to redesign how a real business operates when intelligent agents, structured memory, workflow orchestration, and human oversight are part of the company from the inside out.

I'm doing that in public-facing pieces of my ecosystem, and I'm doing it inside messy, regulated, operationally demanding environments where theory gets punched in the face by reality.

There are plenty of people talking about AI from a safe distance. Fewer are actually trying to wire it into live operations where customers are real, compliance matters, mistakes cost money, and ambiguity shows up every single day. That's the difference between commentary and construction. I'm interested in construction.

Cloud Title is the most grounded example. It's a real Florida title company. We use Qualia as our production platform. We recently adopted Qualia Clear. We have a small team. We close real transactions. We deal with real files, real clients, real agents, real deadlines, real exceptions, and real consequences when something gets missed. That makes it the perfect proving ground.

Let me say this clearly: Cloud Title is not some fully autonomous AI title company. We're not there. Not even close.

We're in the build. We're in the phase where you can see the future but still have to walk through the messy middle to get there. We're testing, refining, identifying what can be automated, what should be automated, what needs oversight, and what still belongs firmly in human hands. That's exactly where most serious companies will live for a while. Not in fantasy. In transition.

At Cloud Title, the category of work I care about most is exception handling and information movement. Title is full of it. Documents come in from different sources. Requirements change. Municipal information is fragmented. Statuses need to be communicated. Questions need to be answered. Follow-up has to happen. Data lives in more than one system. And too much of the work still depends on a human noticing, remembering, checking, emailing, routing, or chasing.

That's a terrible long-term design.

Humans are capable of judgment, trust-building, calming down a nervous seller, explaining a difficult issue to an agent, spotting nuance, and making a decision when the facts are incomplete. Those are high-value human functions. Remembering to send the second update, pulling status from one system to another, watching for predictable exceptions, drafting repetitive communication, routing a task to the right next step, flagging missing items—that's exactly the kind of work intelligent systems should own.

So one of the things I'm building right now is a layer of intelligence around operations. Not a flashy demo. A working layer. That includes workflow automations outside of Clear. It includes experiments connecting operational data to marketing and follow-up systems. It includes the beginning of an agent framework that can bridge what happens in production with what should happen in communication, reporting, relationship management, and business development. In plain English: if something important happens in the operating system, I want the right downstream action to happen without five humans remembering what comes next.

That sounds obvious. In most businesses, it still doesn't happen.

I'm also building around one of the ugliest but most valuable opportunities in title and real estate services: searches, retrieval, and structured information gathering. Local lien searches are a perfect example. In too many markets, this work is fragmented, manual, dependent on different websites, different municipal rules, different interfaces, different turnaround times, and different human habits. It's exactly the kind of ugly, repetitive, error-prone work that most people tolerate because it's always been ugly, repetitive, and error-prone.

I don't accept that. If a process is ugly and repetitive, that's not a reason to keep it human. That's a reason to redesign it.

So we're building toward automated and semi-automated approaches for lien search work and related workflows. Some of that means orchestration. Some means data capture. Some means knowing when to hand off to a human. True automation in the real world is rarely one giant switch. It's more often a sequence of smaller wins: reduce clicks, reduce wait time, reduce handoffs, reduce missed items, reduce dependency on tribal knowledge.

That last one matters a lot. Tribal knowledge is one of the hidden killers in small and midsize businesses. One person knows where something is. One person knows how a certain municipality behaves. One person knows which exception tends to show up in a certain type of file. That may look efficient from the outside. It's not. It's fragile. Part of what I'm building is an operating model that captures process intelligence before it walks out the door, gets buried, or becomes impossible to scale.

That's one side of the laboratory. The other side is OpenClaw.

OpenClaw is where I'm pushing beyond simple AI assistance into something structural: a multi-agent operating environment. Not one chatbot. Not one clever interface. A team architecture.

The reason is simple. Businesses aren't made of one task. They're made of many roles, many responsibilities, many flows of information, many decisions, many dependencies, many kinds of work. If your mental model of AI is still one chat window, you're already behind the architecture that's coming.

In OpenClaw, I'm building a workforce model made up of specialized agents. Some handle strategy. Some handle research. Some handle content. Some handle technical implementation. Some are tied to specific projects. Some are more general. Some need continuity and memory. Some should remain narrow and stateless. Some can be trusted more than others. Some need hard boundaries.

That last sentence may sound technical. It's actually managerial.

This is why I keep saying the future isn't just about using AI. It's about managing AI. When you start working with multiple agents, you run into the same questions you'd run into with human teams, except faster and in a more explicit form. Who owns what? Who should have memory? What instructions are permanent and what are temporary? What gets escalated? What gets approved? What context belongs at the company level, the project level, the role level, or only in a single task? How do you keep an agent from drifting? How do you verify that what was done matches what was asked?

OpenClaw is a working education in digital management. I'm learning, in real time, what it takes to run a digital workforce with enough order that it becomes useful rather than chaotic.

Some of what's working is already clear. Specialization works. Role clarity works. Project-scoped context works better than bloated general context. Memory matters more than most people realize. Governance matters even more.

When an agent has a defined role, clear instructions, bounded context, and a known output standard, quality improves dramatically. When you get lazy and give broad, vague, blended instructions, performance drops, drift increases, and the results start to look like what most people currently experience with AI: impressive in moments, unreliable over time. That's not because AI is useless. It's because poor management creates poor output.

Some of what's hard is equally clear. Infrastructure matters. Naming matters. File structure matters. Memory location matters. Session design matters. Model selection matters. Prompt design matters. Failure recovery matters. A single weak assumption in architecture can create hours of confusion later. Most people still underestimate what it means to build a serious agent-powered business. They think the breakthrough is the model. It's not. The model matters, but the real breakthrough is operational design.

I have no interest in pretending this is turnkey. It's emerging. There are moments when it feels like the future just showed up in the room. There are other moments when you realize you're one bad assumption away from drift, duplication, or wasted effort. The internet didn't show up fully formed either. What encourages me isn't that every piece works perfectly. What encourages me is that the pattern is unmistakable. Once you see agents do real work inside a structured system, even imperfectly, you can't unsee where this is headed.

I'm also building around education, advisory, and translation. I've always been at my best when I'm both building and teaching. I did it in the early internet era. I did it in real estate. I'm doing it again now. AI Training Academy, my broader entrepreneur-facing work, and the content I publish all come from the same conviction: most entrepreneurs don't need more AI theory. They need translation.

They need someone to tell them what matters, what doesn't, where to start, what to ignore, what's real, what's hype, what's worth building, and how to avoid drowning in tools.

That's a huge gap right now. A lot of AI content is either too shallow to be useful or too technical to be adopted. One side says, "Look what this tool can do." The other disappears into abstractions and architecture diagrams that most business owners will never use. What's missing is a practical bridge from curiosity to operational redesign. That bridge is one of the things I'm building.

That's why I care about building in public. Not recklessly. Not performatively. But honestly. Here's what we tried. Here's what worked. Here's what broke. Here's what I'd do differently. Here's where the human still matters. Here's what the agent can now own. Here's the system I'd never trust without review. Here's the one I trust more every week.

That kind of honesty builds authority faster than polished storytelling ever will. It also keeps me honest with myself. One danger in a frontier market is that you start believing your own positioning faster than your systems deserve. I have no interest in doing that. I'd rather be slightly understated and structurally right than loudly impressive and operationally hollow.

I'm not writing this book from the standpoint of a theorist. I'm writing as an operator with skin in the game. I have clients. I have payroll. I have regulated workflows. I have a real brand. I have real stakes. And I'm using those environments as live laboratories to figure out what an AI-native business actually looks like as it's being born.

The three tracks reinforce each other. Cloud Title gives me a real operating company in a demanding industry. OpenClaw gives me the architecture playground to push the frontier. The training and advisory side forces me to translate what I'm learning into language, frameworks, and decisions other entrepreneurs can actually use.

That combination keeps me from drifting into either extreme. I can't become a pure theorist, because I'm building in the real world. I can't get so buried in operational detail that I lose the larger pattern, because I'm constantly stepping back to teach what I'm learning.

And let me say something plainly. The final prize here isn't just efficiency.

Efficiency is part of it. Lower labor intensity. Faster execution. Better routing. Better visibility. Fewer dropped balls. Those all matter. But the bigger opportunity is enterprise redesign. When a business learns to combine humans, software, agents, memory, governance, and workflow intelligence into one operating system, it stops behaving like a traditional small company. It starts behaving like something larger than its headcount. That changes valuation. Resilience. Scalability. The founder's role. What becomes possible.

I've been chasing that shift my entire career, whether I had the words for it or not. When I built early internet infrastructure, I was helping small businesses gain capabilities that belonged to larger companies. When I built systems-heavy real estate operations, I was trying to industrialize what had been too dependent on individual chaos. What I'm doing now is the next logical step: giving entrepreneurs a way to build with capabilities that used to require layers of staff, layers of management, and layers of cost. This time, part of the workforce is digital. Memory can be structured. Execution can be distributed across agents. Oversight can be designed instead of improvised. A company can start to become intelligent by design.

That's what I'm building right now. Not perfectly. Not all at once. Not with some fantasy that the machine replaces the human. A hybrid future. Human-led. Agent-powered. Governed. Iterative. Commercial. Useful.

And I'm doing it while the window is still open. The early movers don't win because they guessed everything right. They win because they got into motion early enough to learn faster than everyone else.

That's why I'm willing to deal with the messy middle. That's why I'm willing to show the work instead of waiting for a polished ending. And that's why the next question matters.

If this shift isn't limited to title, or real estate, or my own laboratory—where else is the same pattern about to play out?

The answer is: almost everywhere.

Chapter 11

Every Industry Has Its 1994 Moment

In 1994, most people were not stupid. They were just pointed in the wrong direction.

They weren't blind. They could see the internet. They just misread what they were seeing. They thought email would replace fax machines. They thought websites would be glorified brochures. They thought the whole thing was interesting, maybe useful, but not structurally important.

The internet was not a better fax machine. It wasn't a digital brochure rack. It wasn't a nicer version of the systems that already existed. It was a new operating layer for commerce, communication, distribution, trust, customer acquisition, and scale.

The entrepreneurs who saw that early didn't just adopt a new tool. They redesigned their businesses around a new reality.

That's what's happening right now with AI agents.

Most industries are still treating AI as an accessory. A writing assistant. A chatbot. A search box with better grammar. Something to help draft emails faster, summarize notes, maybe polish a proposal. That's the equivalent of using the early internet to send prettier faxes.

What matters is not whether AI can help someone inside the current model. What matters is whether the current model itself is about to be rebuilt.

Every industry has a moment when the old assumptions quietly stop being true. The incumbents don't notice immediately because the familiar version still seems to work. Revenue still comes in. Clients still call. Staff still does the work the same way they did last year. The software stack is annoying but tolerable. The inefficiency is expensive but invisible because everyone has the same inefficiency.

Then the ground shifts.

Not all at once. At first it looks minor. A faster process here. A lower-cost competitor there. A startup with weird economics. A boutique operator that somehow responds faster, ships quicker, produces more with fewer people, and keeps improving every month.

That's usually the first sign.

When I look across industries today, I don't see one AI future. I see six or seven different 1994 moments happening in parallel. They don't all look the same. The regulations are different. The risks are different. The human stakes are different. The adoption curve is different. But the pattern is the same.

A new layer of capability has arrived. Most people are using it to decorate the old model. A few people are using it to replace the old model. Those are the people who will own the next decade.

Let me show you what I mean.

— — —

I'll start with legal because on the surface it looks protected.

Law firms love to believe they're insulated by complexity. In fairness, some of that is true. Legal work is nuanced. Stakes are high. Judgment matters. Reputation matters. A bad decision can cost a client a business, a deal, a freedom interest, or a fortune.

So when lawyers hear AI, many of them go to the same place: useful for research maybe, dangerous for real work. That sounds reasonable. It's also exactly how industries talk right before they get reorganized.

The wrong question in legal is whether AI can replace lawyers. It can't replace good lawyers in the way some people imagine — and more importantly, that's not the economically interesting question.

The right question: how much of a legal business is actually lawyer judgment, and how much of it is document assembly, pattern recognition, review, issue spotting, drafting, workflow routing, intake, follow-up, compliance monitoring, deadline management, evidence organization, and client communication?

In a lot of firms, a huge amount of the work surrounding the legal brain is process, not judgment.

Picture a firm where every new client inquiry is triaged by an intake agent that knows the firm's service lines, conflict-check rules, ideal client profile, and urgency logic. It asks the right questions, collects the right documents, routes the matter correctly, and flags missing information before a human ever touches the file. Add a matter-prep agent that assembles a first-pass chronology, extracts key entities from contracts, identifies likely issue categories, drafts internal memos, compares clauses against a preferred playbook, and alerts the attorney where the risk actually lives. Add deadline monitoring, discovery organization, client communication, and billing support that turns activity into cleaner time entries and fewer forgotten billables.

None of that eliminates the lawyer. It changes the economics of the firm.

The pioneer move in legal is straightforward: stop asking where AI can help the lawyer, and start asking how to build a firm where lawyers spend more time on actual lawyering. The best firms will be able to handle more matters per attorney, respond faster, maintain cleaner files, and create a noticeably better client experience.

They'll call faster. They'll miss less. They'll surface issues earlier. They'll onboard more cleanly. They'll turn around work with less internal chaos.

That's how category shifts usually appear in the beginning. Not as science fiction. As operational unfairness.

— — —

Healthcare has its own version of this, and the stakes are higher.

Healthcare is one of the most burdened administrative systems in the modern economy. Brilliant clinicians are surrounded by paperwork, fragmented records, insurance friction, repetitive documentation, scheduling failures, follow-up gaps, medication confusion, compliance requirements, coding headaches, and broken communication between patients and providers.

In other words, the industry is drowning in process drag. That makes it a large target.

The conversation people keep having — will AI replace doctors? — is the wrong one. The meaningful question is how much clinical capacity is being wasted by non-clinical friction.

A healthcare organization's 1994 moment begins when it stops viewing AI as a diagnostic novelty and starts viewing it as an operating system for administrative relief, patient flow, documentation support, and continuity.

Imagine a primary care practice where an intake agent gathers patient history before the visit in a structured, useful format instead of forcing the patient to scribble half-legible answers on a clipboard. A visit-support agent listens during the appointment, produces a structured note draft, flags missing documentation, suggests coding support, and prepares follow-up instructions in plain English. A medication and care-plan agent checks whether patients actually understood what they were told, reminds them what to do next, and surfaces drop-off risk before noncompliance becomes a problem. A referral coordination agent chases documents, confirms receipt, schedules next steps, and closes loops that today stay open for weeks.

That's not replacing the physician. That's reclaiming physician time, reducing burnout, improving patient experience, and tightening the reliability of care. The same applies in specialty care, physical therapy, dental, surgery centers, home health, behavioral health, and revenue-cycle operations.

In many healthcare settings, the bottleneck isn't demand. It's throughput and friction. The pioneer move is to target the invisible waste around the clinician — not the sacred center of judgment, but the burden around it.

And let me say something that applies across all regulated industries.

The presence of regulation doesn't eliminate the opportunity. It increases the value of getting the system right. When people tell me an industry is too regulated to change quickly, I hear that the winners will be the ones disciplined enough to design with guardrails. That's not a reason to sit still. That's a reason the prize will be bigger.

— — —

Financial services is another obvious 1994 moment.

Banks, lenders, insurance carriers, RIAs, wealth managers, and brokerages all have some version of the same problem: too much human labor wrapped around repeatable processes that still require trust, documentation, judgment, and compliance.

A lot of financial firms are already using AI in bits and pieces. Meeting summaries. Marketing copy. Chat support. Some fraud monitoring. Fine. Better than nothing. But that's not the real shift.

The real shift happens when a financial firm starts redesigning the client journey and internal workflow around agent systems instead of departments and handoffs.

Take a mortgage operation. In many shops, borrowers get chased for documents manually. Conditions are explained poorly. Process visibility is weak. Loan officers spend time babysitting tasks that should never require their attention. Processors drown in follow-up. Underwriters become bottlenecks because files arrive dirty.

Now imagine an agent-powered model. A borrower-onboarding agent explains the process, gathers documents, checks for missing pieces, and nudges intelligently rather than through generic reminders. A file-quality agent reviews submissions for completeness before they move downstream. A communication agent keeps the borrower informed in plain language. A milestone agent alerts the human team only when something meaningful changes or intervention is required. Done properly, that doesn't reduce trust — it increases trust because the borrower finally knows what's happening.

Same story in wealth management. The best advisors aren't going away. But everything around the advisor is being repriced. Client onboarding, risk-profile collection, meeting prep, plan recap, review scheduling, compliance logging, portfolio commentary drafts, and life-event monitoring can all be materially improved with agent systems.

The pioneer move in financial services is to preserve the human center of trust while industrializing the surrounding workflow with unusual precision.

This is where people get confused. They think moving early means making the business colder, more robotic, more detached. I think the opposite is true. A properly designed agent-powered business often feels more human, because the humans in it are no longer buried under low-value process work. The advisor has more attention. The lender has more clarity. The relationship manager has more time to actually manage the relationship.

That's the difference between automation done to cut corners and automation done to create capacity.

— — —

Logistics might be the easiest place to see the shift because the inefficiency is already measurable.

If you move freight, manage warehouses, coordinate dispatch, run delivery networks, or handle supply chain operations, you already live in a world of timing, routing, exceptions, costs, delays, and constant decisions under pressure.

A logistics company's future advantage will come less from owning assets and more from how intelligently it can orchestrate them. Loads need to be matched. Routes need to be adjusted. Exceptions need to be identified early. Customers need proactive communication. Documentation needs to move fast. Margins need to be protected.

These are live systems, not one-time tasks. This is why AI agents matter more than one-off automations here. A workflow automation can trigger a step. An agent can monitor, reason, escalate, summarize, and adapt inside boundaries.

Imagine a dispatch agent watching for route disruption, weather, driver availability, delivery windows, and historical delay patterns — not replacing the operations leader, but reducing the number of surprises that hit too late. A customer communication agent that updates clients automatically when a shipment moves, stalls, reroutes, or risks missing a milestone. An exception-resolution agent that identifies likely paperwork gaps, customs snags, dwell risks, or chargeback issues before they become expensive messes.

The pioneer move in logistics is to turn operations from reactive management into intelligent supervision. Logistics companies don't typically die from lack of demand. They die from accumulated disorder — margins chewed up by preventable errors, miscommunication, overtime, rework, penalties, and poor coordination. The companies that build agent awareness into their operating layer won't just be faster. They'll be calmer. And calmer systems make more money.

— — —

Education is another sector where people are underestimating what's coming.

Most conversations about AI in education get hijacked immediately by cheating, plagiarism, and whether students will use AI to avoid doing the work. Those are real issues — and also too narrow.

The deeper shift is that education has been constrained for decades by the economics of one-to-many instruction, uneven personalization, teacher overload, and administrative inefficiency. A great teacher with thirty students can't tutor every student individually every day. A course creator can't easily adapt one curriculum into twenty personalized pathways. A training company can't provide infinite support without infinite payroll.

That used to be a hard constraint. Now it's becoming less true.

The 1994 moment in education is the arrival of scalable personalization. A strong educational business or institution can use agent systems to create guided practice, personalized reinforcement, adaptive tutoring, assignment support, feedback loops, progress visibility, parent communication, and administrative follow-through at a level that previously required far more staff.

The best teachers become more valuable because the delivery model around them improves.

In corporate training, this becomes even more obvious. Most companies run training badly — information gets delivered once, retention is weak, follow-through is inconsistent, and nobody really knows what stuck. An agent-powered training model can onboard employees, reinforce lessons, quiz for comprehension, provide contextual reminders, escalate confusion, track progress, and adapt the pace to the learner. That's not a small improvement. That's a different category of capability.

The pioneer move in education is to stop treating AI as a threat to content integrity and start treating it as a force multiplier for coaching, personalization, and continuity. Students get more support. Teachers get relief. Administrators get better visibility. Training organizations deliver transformation, not just information.

— — —

Now let me come closer to home.

Real estate services are having their 1994 moment, and most of the industry still doesn't realize how broad that statement is.

When people hear real estate and AI, they usually think listing descriptions, social media posts, CMA assistance, chatbots, or better lead follow-up. Those things are fine. They're not the real story.

Real estate services are full of fragmented workflows, human coordination burdens, slow follow-up, paperwork drag, vendor handoffs, inconsistent client communication, and knowledge trapped inside experienced operators. That includes brokerages, teams, title companies, mortgage companies, transaction coordination, property management, inspections, and ancillary service providers.

I know this world well enough to tell you that the hidden cost is not just labor. It's delay, inconsistency, and dropped attention.

The 1994 moment here isn't a smarter marketing assistant. It's the shift from personality-driven operations to system-driven operations with human oversight.

Most real estate teams still depend on a few strong people to remember everything, chase everything, notice everything, and keep everything moving. When those people are great, the business looks smooth. When they leave, the business discovers it had a hero dependency, not a system.

Imagine a team where inquiry handling, lead qualification, listing intake, showing coordination, inspection tracking, contract-to-close communication, and post-close follow-up are supported by agents that know the playbook, the tone, the sequencing, and when to escalate. That doesn't eliminate the agent. It sharpens the agent.

Now take title — which is one reason I'm so focused on what we're building at Cloud Title. Title is a perfect example of a legacy service business that still contains huge amounts of manual coordination, issue spotting, communication dependency, and workflow complexity. Some of that absolutely requires experienced humans. Some of it doesn't.

We're not fully AI-automated. We're in the early stages of the transformation. We use Qualia as our core production platform, we've recently adopted Qualia Clear, and we're actively building workflow automations, exploring a proprietary platform direction, and testing related systems around transaction coordination, lien searches, CRM connectivity, and process intelligence.

I don't want to write fantasy. But I can already see clearly where this industry is going.

The title company of the future won't be a group of people pushing files through a legacy system and sending update emails manually all day. It'll be a coordinated operating environment where humans handle judgment, exceptions, relationship trust, curative strategy, and final accountability while agent systems support intake, status movement, document handling, routine communication, issue flagging, follow-up, reporting, and internal visibility.

The pioneer move in real estate services is to redesign around flow. Not around software procurement. Not around shiny demos. Around flow. Where does work stall? Where does communication break? Where do customers get confused? Where do staff members duplicate effort? Where does important knowledge live only in one person's head? Those are the redesign starting points.

— — —

Accounting deserves a quick stop because it's quietly one of the most obvious candidates for structural change.

Bookkeeping, month-end close, reconciliations, document requests, categorization review, client follow-up, variance explanations, tax document collection, audit prep, internal controls monitoring, and reporting support all live in an environment where trust matters and routine is everywhere.

The pioneer move in accounting isn't to pretend AI is the CPA. It's to build a firm where the CPA is no longer buried under the machinery surrounding the CPA.

Same theme. Different vertical.

When the same pattern keeps appearing across unrelated industries, you're not looking at a niche tool trend. You're looking at a broad economic shift.

— — —

That's exactly what happened in the early internet era.

At first, people talked about websites. But websites were never the real story. The real story was that distribution changed. Discovery changed. Customer acquisition changed. Commerce changed. Support changed. Publishing changed. Speed changed. Global reach changed. The visible artifact distracted people from the underlying reorganization.

Today, the visible artifact is ChatGPT.

That's why so many people are still underestimating what's happening. They think the story is the interface. It's not.

The story is that intelligence, execution support, monitoring, drafting, and workflow reasoning are becoming more available, more affordable, and more deployable than at any time in business history. That changes what a small company can do. It changes how fast a startup can become dangerous. It changes what headcount means. It changes the design of service businesses. It changes what clients will expect once a few pioneers reset the bar.

And that last part is critical.

In every industry, pioneers don't just gain efficiency. They change customer expectations.

Once one law firm becomes dramatically more responsive, clients start noticing slower firms. Once one healthcare practice becomes clearer and easier to navigate, patients notice the chaos elsewhere. Once one lender creates a borrower experience that feels transparent and organized, the old black-box process starts to feel insulting. Once one training company provides real continuity and personalized reinforcement, passive content libraries feel dead. Once one real estate service provider communicates with uncommon consistency and speed, everyone else starts looking sloppy.

That's how the window closes. Not when everyone understands the technology. When customer expectations move.

That's why every industry's 1994 moment is also every industry's warning shot.

There's still time to move early in a lot of sectors. But "early" doesn't mean first person to hear about AI — that phase is over. Early now means first serious operator in your category to redesign the business around it.

Hearing about a wave doesn't matter. Building into it does.

— — —

So what does "Twice Ahead" actually look like if you're an entrepreneur inside one of these industries?

You stop asking, "How can I use AI a little?"

You start asking, "If I were rebuilding this company today from scratch, knowing what agent systems can now do, what would I design differently?"

You identify the trust core of the business — the part that must remain human-led. You identify the workflow shell around it — the part that can be monitored, drafted, routed, explained, organized, checked, followed up, summarized, or escalated by agents.

You stop treating your current org chart as sacred. You stop assuming every repetitive task deserves a human owner. You stop confusing software adoption with operating model redesign.

You start thinking in roles, responsibilities, handoffs, thresholds, memory, governance, and escalation.

You build one real system. Then another. Then another.

That's how a pioneer advantage is actually built. Not through one giant leap. Through a series of live operational redesigns that compound.

I've seen enough of these cycles to tell you that the people who wait for certainty almost always miss the best part of the curve. In 1994, most people wanted proof before they moved. By the time the proof was obvious, the smartest opportunities were already being claimed. Domain names were being taken. Hosting companies were scaling. Ecommerce infrastructure was forming. Search dynamics were emerging. Positioning advantages were being established. The people who moved while it still looked messy built a lead that was hard to erase later.

This cycle won't be identical. But the pattern rhymes so loudly that I can hear it from across industries.

The companies that move now, with discipline, will build operating advantages their competitors will struggle to understand, much less match. Not because they have magical AI. Because they redesigned sooner.

That's the point of this book. Not to impress you with trends. To get you to act while the window is still open.

Because whatever industry you're in, someone in your space is already building the version of the business that makes the current version look old.

The only question is whether that will be you.

And that brings us to the final issue — the one that matters most.

What do you do now? How do you move without creating chaos? How do you avoid getting distracted by noise, vapor, tools, and busywork? How do you take a business that was built for one era and begin redesigning it for another in the next ninety days?

That's where we're going next.

Seeing the pattern matters. But building on it before the crowd does is what changes everything.

Chapter 12

The Window Is Open.
It Won't Stay Open.

I 've seen what a real technology window looks like when it first cracks open.

In 1994, most business owners didn't think they were ignoring the future. They thought they were being sensible. Why would I need a website? Isn't email just a faster fax machine? Who's going to buy anything from a computer screen?

Those weren't stupid people. Some were smart. Some were successful. Some had much more money than I did, better credentials, bigger staffs, and more credibility in the marketplace.

What they didn't have was accurate pattern recognition. They misread the magnitude of the shift.

I remember how narrow the conversation was. Businesses thought in terms of isolated tools — email, a website, maybe an electronic catalog. Very few understood that the internet wasn't going to be one more marketing channel bolted onto the side of the business. It was going to become the business infrastructure itself.

That was the mistake. And that mistake created one of the greatest entrepreneurial wealth transfers of my lifetime.

The people who moved early got cheap distribution, cheap attention, cheap experimentation, and cheap market share. They got to make mistakes before the world was crowded. They got to build customer habits before those habits became expensive to influence. They got to look smarter than they were because the field was still empty.

Then the window narrowed.

By the time the broader market understood what the web really was, the easiest advantages were gone. Domains were taken. Categories were forming. Infrastructure standards were rising. Competition was showing up with money. What had been an open frontier started becoming an actual market.

That's where we are now with AI agents.

Not with AI in the general sense. That conversation is already crowded. Everyone knows what ChatGPT is. Everyone has seen image generation. Everyone has heard some version of "AI is changing everything." That phase is over.

The open window isn't around awareness. It's around structure.

Very few companies have actually redesigned themselves around agent-powered work. Very few founders have built even one real AI role with decision boundaries, memory, escalation rules, and measurable output. Even fewer have done it in a way that compounds.

That's why the window is still open. And that's why it won't stay open for long.

People hear that and assume I'm trying to create urgency for effect. I'm not. I'm telling you how these cycles actually work.

The early stage of a shift always feels longer than it is. The tools are inconsistent. The demos are better than the deployments. The terminology is confusing. Hype artists get loud. Serious operators stay cautious. And because the change is uneven, most people assume they still have plenty of time.

They don't.

What compresses the window isn't the headline cycle. It's the learning cycle.

Once a certain number of companies begin building real agent-powered workflows, they start accumulating advantages that don't show up on the surface right away. They learn where human review matters and where it doesn't. They learn which tasks are stable enough for automation and which ones need tighter controls. They learn how to structure prompts, approvals, escalations, and audit trails. They train their people to work with digital coworkers instead of treating

AI like a novelty.

That learning compounds.

The latecomer can buy software. The latecomer can't buy five hundred days of accumulated operational learning.

That's the part most people miss. The real moat isn't the model. It isn't even the software stack. The real moat is the organization that has already learned how to think in workflows, roles, exceptions, and machine-augmented execution. The moat is managerial. It's cultural. It's architectural.

And once a competitor builds that muscle, you're not catching them by subscribing to the same tools they use. You're catching them by going through the same pain they already went through a year earlier.

That's why I keep coming back to the phrase twice ahead.

In 1994, being ahead meant seeing that the internet would matter before the average business owner believed it. Today, being twice ahead means seeing that AI itself isn't the point. The point is the redesign of the company.

Most people are still asking, "How do I use AI?"

The better question is, "How do I build a business that gets stronger every month because more of its work is being handled by intelligent systems under human oversight?"

That's a different game. And games like that reward movement, not spectatorship.

Let me make this practical.

If you're still using AI only for writing emails, summarizing articles, brainstorming headlines, or cleaning up documents, you're not behind in the absolute sense. Those are useful things. I use them too. But you're still operating at the surface.

The window I'm talking about belongs to the people who go one level deeper and begin assigning work. Not "help me think about this." Do this. Research this every Monday. Review these files and flag exceptions. Draft this response and route it to me for approval. Monitor this data source and alert me only when the pattern changes. Follow up until this moves to the next stage.

That's where the change begins to matter.

At Cloud Title, I'm living this in real time. Not as a polished case study — as a messy build. We're still early. The transformation isn't complete. But that's exactly the point. The value is in building while the window is still open, not in pretending you waited until everything was clean and obvious. With OpenClaw, I'm building multi-agent infrastructure and learning firsthand where orchestration works, where memory matters, where governance matters, and where complexity gets out of hand if you're sloppy. That live experimentation has only reinforced my conviction: this isn't a someday shift. It's an operating shift already underway.

The mistake now isn't skepticism. Healthy skepticism is fine. The mistake is delay disguised as sophistication.

I've seen a lot of that lately. Founders saying they're "watching the space." Executives saying they're "developing a strategy." Leadership teams holding workshops about AI transformation while no actual workflow has been redesigned. People spending six months comparing platforms before deploying a single useful agent.

That's not strategy. That's avoidance wearing a blazer.

Here's what I'd tell any serious entrepreneur right now.

Don't begin by trying to transform the whole company. Don't begin with an AI committee. Don't begin by asking which model is best this week. And don't begin with the vague goal of "becoming an AI company." That phrase means nothing operationally.

Begin with one workflow that matters. One.

If you can't identify one workflow in your business that's repetitive, time-sensitive, partially rules-based, and economically meaningful, you're not looking hard enough. Every business has them. Lead intake. Customer onboarding. Follow-up. Document review. Proposal drafting. Invoice chasing. Exception monitoring. Compliance checks.

Pick one that happens often enough to matter and is painful enough that you'd feel the relief if it improved.

Then spend the first thirty days doing something most companies skip: map the work honestly. Not the version in the SOP binder. The real version. What triggers it? Who touches it? What information is needed? What decisions are made? What goes wrong? Where does it stall? What exceptions are common?

This is where a lot of founders get impatient. They want to jump straight to the tool.

Bad idea. If your workflow is muddy, your automation will be muddy. If your process is full of tribal knowledge, hidden exceptions, and inconsistent judgment, an agent will expose that very quickly.

Good. That's not failure. That's the diagnosis.

The first thirty days aren't about sophistication. They're about clarity. You're choosing the workflow. Naming the owner. Establishing the baseline — the current cycle time, the current error rate, the current handoff points, the current cost in human attention. You're deciding what success would look like ninety days from now. Not perfection. Improvement.

Maybe the workflow moves 30 percent faster. Maybe the owner gets five hours a week back. Maybe response time drops from twenty-four hours to two. Maybe missed follow-up falls by half.

It doesn't matter which metric you choose as long as it's real. What matters is that this stops being a philosophy discussion and becomes an operating discipline.

During that same first month, define the guardrails. What can the agent do on its own? What must be reviewed by a human? What data can it access? What tone or brand rules must it follow? When does it escalate? What gets logged?

Don't make this complicated. Just make it explicit. A business becomes dangerous with AI when it gives systems implicit authority without explicit boundaries.

The second thirty days are where your first autonomous hire starts to become real.

I call it an autonomous hire because that framing forces the right questions. If this were a new team member, what role would they own? What would you expect from them every day? What would success look like? What mistakes would be tolerable? What mistakes would be unacceptable? Who manages them?

Once you frame it that way, you stop treating AI like magic and start treating it like workforce design. That's the mindset shift.

In days thirty-one through sixty, deploy a narrow agent into the chosen workflow. Narrow wins early. The goal isn't to create a genius assistant who can do everything. The goal is to create a reliable operator who can do one job well enough to save time, improve speed, or increase consistency.

Maybe it's a follow-up agent that drafts responses, routes them for approval, and logs next actions. Maybe it's a research agent that monitors a market and flags only what matters. Maybe it's an intake agent that turns incoming requests into structured records and queues work correctly. Maybe it's a document agent that reads files, checks for required elements, and flags exceptions.

Simple is better than impressive.

This is also the phase where you need to resist one of the most common mistakes in the AI cycle: giving human beings unclear instructions about how to work with the new system. If your team thinks the agent is either a toy or a threat, you're going to get distorted results. Some people will ignore it. Some will overtrust it. Some will sabotage it quietly because they think it's coming for their job.

That's why leadership matters. Tell the truth. The system is here to take friction out of the workflow, not to create a science project. Human judgment still matters. Human review still matters. Accountability still belongs to people. But the work itself is going to change.

By this stage, you should also be logging everything you can learn from. Where does the agent perform well? Where does it stumble? What instructions produce bad output? What exceptions recur? Those aren't annoyances. They're training data for your operating model.

Then comes the third thirty days.

Days sixty-one through ninety are where most businesses either begin compounding or begin drifting. If the first deployment shows promise, don't celebrate too early. Tighten it. Document the role, the rules, the escalation points, the KPIs, and who owns the workflow.

Create a short weekly review. Fifteen minutes is enough. What worked? What failed? What changed? What needs adjustment? What should be promoted from experiment to standard process?

That weekly rhythm matters because it's how AI stops being an event and becomes management.

Then add one adjacent layer. Not five. One.

This is where you begin to feel what an agent-powered company can become. Your first agent took one slice of work. Now you add a second function around it. Maybe the intake agent triggers the follow-up agent. Maybe the research agent feeds the content agent. Maybe the document checker routes issues to a human closer with a clean summary.

This is where compounding begins. One role starts helping another role. One workflow starts reducing friction in a neighboring workflow. One source of structured data starts making another process more valuable.

That's when you stop seeing AI as a series of tools and start seeing it as an architecture.

Now let me tell you what to ignore during these ninety days, because this matters just as much.

Ignore the endless debate over which model won the benchmark war this week. Ignore the flood of content from people who've never operated a business but suddenly have opinions about agentic transformation. Ignore vanity experiments that look great in demos and die in production. Ignore the urge to automate low-value tasks just because they're easy. And ignore anyone telling you that you need a complete AI transformation roadmap before you can start. You don't.

What you need is one real workflow, one accountable owner, one controlled deployment, and one cadence of review. That's enough to begin.

Also ignore the fantasy that you can install an AI layer on top of managerial sloppiness and somehow get excellence. You won't. If your team is unclear, your systems are inconsistent, your standards are invisible, and your data is a mess, AI won't save you. It will expose you.

Good. That's useful. But be honest about it.

A lot of businesses are going to discover over the next three years that their real bottleneck was never labor cost. It was operational ambiguity. The businesses that win will use AI to force clarity.

One more warning: don't confuse velocity with chaos.

Moving now doesn't mean flailing. It means sequencing correctly. Every agent needs an owner — a person, not a committee. Every workflow needs a measurable outcome — a real one, not "improve efficiency." Every deployment needs a fallback. Every agent needs clear authority limits. And every experiment needs a review date, because nothing should run forever just because it was set up once.

That's how you avoid building a haunted house of half-working automations nobody understands. I've seen that movie too.

Here's what I believe is going to happen over the next few years. The first group of winners won't be the biggest companies. They'll be the fastest learners. Some will be small. Some won't look impressive at first glance. But underneath, they'll be redesigning how work gets done — capturing data better, serving clients faster, routing decisions more intelligently, operating with leaner teams and greater output.

By the time the larger market notices, those companies will have a structural lead.

This is exactly what happened in the early internet era. The businesses that moved first didn't all look glamorous. Some looked strange. Some looked too early. But the operators inside them were accumulating a new kind of competence while everyone else was still debating the premise.

That's the real prize now. Competence before consensus.

That's what the open window offers you. Not certainty. Not safety. Not a guarantee. An opening. A chance to build the managerial, architectural, and cultural capability of an agent-powered business before that capability becomes table stakes.

If I were sitting across the table from you over dinner and you asked me what to do next, I'd make it very simple.

In the next seven days, choose the workflow. In the next fourteen days, map it honestly. In the next thirty days, define the metrics and guardrails. In the next sixty days, deploy the first narrow autonomous role. In the next ninety days, review it, tighten it, and connect it to one adjacent workflow.

Do that, and you're no longer talking about AI. You're building with it.

That distinction is going to separate the next decade's winners from the next decade's conference attendees.

The window is open right now. That's the good news.

The bad news — if you want to call it that — is the same as it was in 1994: open windows don't stay open just because smart people wish they had more time. Markets learn. Competitors adapt. Tools improve. Standards rise. Costs of inaction accumulate quietly and then all at once.

You can still be early. But early has a shelf life.

At some point, what's now initiative becomes catch-up. What's now a strategic edge becomes an industry requirement. The companies that acted while the field was still loose will have built systems, habits, and data advantages that the latecomers will mistake for luck.

It won't be luck. It will be timing matched with action.

That's how pioneer windows work. And that's why I wrote this book.

Not to convince you that AI exists — you already know that. Not to impress you with terminology — that's useless. Not to sell you the fantasy of a push-button autonomous company — that's nonsense.

I wrote it to help you see the pattern clearly enough to act while action still matters most.

Build the first role. Design the first workflow. Put governance around it. Learn faster than the market. Then do it again.

That's how you become twice ahead.

And if you do it right, one day people will look at the company you built and assume it was obvious where all of this was going.

It never is. It only looks obvious later.

Right now, it still looks early.

Good. That's exactly the moment you want.

Appendix A
The Pioneer's Self-Assessment Diagnostic

M ost business owners don't have an AI strategy problem. They have an honesty problem.

They say they're "using AI" because someone on the team writes emails with ChatGPT or generates social media posts. That's not useless, but it's not transformation. It's surface-level adoption.

This diagnostic helps you evaluate where your business actually sits on the AI maturity curve right now. Not where you hope it sits. Where it truly sits.

The goal: identify your current level, score your organization honestly, and know what your next move should be.

Prefer to take this digitally? An interactive version of this diagnostic is available at **twiceahead.com/diagnostic**, where you'll receive a personalized score breakdown and customized next steps.

How to Use This Diagnostic

Rate your business across the ten categories below.

Use this scoring scale for each category:

0 points — Not started

1 point — Minimal or inconsistent

2 points — Functional but limited

3 points — Strong and repeatable

4 points — Advanced and strategic

5 points — Agent-powered and operationalized

Write down your score for each category, then total your points at the end.

Don't overthink it. The point isn't perfection. It's clarity.

1. Leadership Understanding

How well does ownership or executive leadership understand the difference between AI tools, workflows, and agents?

0 — Leadership hasn't seriously engaged with AI.

1 — Leadership sees AI mostly as a writing or research tool.

2 — Leadership understands AI may affect operations, but thinking is still vague.

3 — Leadership understands AI can improve workflows and reduce manual work.

4 — Leadership is actively thinking in terms of role design, orchestration, and digital workers.

5 — Leadership is building the company around an agent-powered operating model.

Your score: _____

2. Workflow Clarity

How clearly has the business mapped its recurring workflows?

0 — Processes mostly live in people's heads.

1 — A few tasks are documented, but workflows are informal.

2 — Some recurring processes are documented, but not end to end.

3 — Core workflows are mapped and repeatable.

4 — The business knows where friction, handoffs, bottlenecks, and errors occur.

5 — Workflows are explicitly designed for human-plus-agent execution.

Your score: _____

3. Data and System Readiness

How accessible is the information required to support AI-assisted work?

0 — Information is scattered across inboxes, spreadsheets, and tribal knowledge.

1 — Some data is digital, but much of it is inconsistent or hard to access.

2 — Core systems exist, but data quality is uneven.

3 — Key information is centralized in business systems.

4 — Data is structured well enough to support automations and AI.

5 — Data, documents, and system access are organized intentionally for agent use.

Your score: _____

4. Current AI Usage

How broadly and consistently is AI being used right now?

0 — No real usage.

1 — One or two people use AI occasionally.

2 — Several people use AI, but mostly for ad hoc tasks.

3 — AI is used regularly across multiple roles.

4 — AI is embedded into recurring work and internal standards.

5 — AI is not an add-on. It's part of daily operations.

Your score: _____

5. Automation Maturity

How much of the business already uses automation, with or without AI?

0 — Almost none.

1 — A few basic automations exist.

2 — Some repetitive administrative tasks are automated.

3 — Multiple workflows use automations across systems.

4 — Automation is treated as an operating discipline.

5 — Automation and AI are integrated into a coordinated execution layer.

Your score: _____

6. Role Design for AI

Has the company identified which roles or role fragments could be handled by AI agents?

0 — No role-based thinking yet.

1 — General curiosity, but no real analysis.

2 — A few tasks have been identified for AI assistance.

3 — Specific roles or role fragments have been broken into repeatable components.

4 — The company is designing specialist digital roles around defined outcomes.

5 — The company actively manages a hybrid org chart of humans, software, and agents.

Your score: _____

7. Governance and Guardrails

How clearly has the business defined boundaries for AI use?

0 — No rules, no guardrails, no review standards.

1 — Informal caution, but nothing documented.

2 — Some review and approval exists for important outputs.

3 — Clear boundaries exist for what AI can do and what requires human approval.

4 — Escalation rules, approval thresholds, and exception handling are defined.

5 — Governance is built into the operating model and trusted by leadership.

Your score: _____

8. Memory and Context Handling

Can your systems preserve context so work improves over time?

0 — No shared memory or retained context.

1 — Teams rely mostly on inboxes, notes, and recollection.

2 — Some documentation exists, but it's fragmented.

3 — Key context is captured in SOPs, CRMs, project tools, or knowledge bases.

4 — Business context is intentionally organized so humans and systems can use it.

5 — Memory architecture is treated as a strategic asset for scale, continuity, and better agent performance.

Your score: _____

9. Measurement and Accountability

How well can you measure whether AI is actually improving the business?

0 — No measurement.

1 — Anecdotal wins only.

2 — A few metrics are observed casually.

3 — AI improvements are measured in time saved, output speed, or quality.

4 — AI initiatives are tied to operational KPIs and business goals.

5 — Each agent or workflow has clear performance expectations, ownership, and review.

Your score: _____

10. Strategic Commitment

How serious is the company about becoming agent-powered?

0 — No real commitment.

1 — Mild interest.

2 — Experiments are happening, but without urgency.

3 — AI is now considered strategically important.

4 — Leadership is investing time, tools, and operating attention.

5 — The business is actively redesigning itself around AI-enabled execution.

Your score: _____

Total Score

Add your ten category scores together.

Total: _____ / 50

What Your Score Means

Level 1: Not Started (0–10)

You're still standing on the shoreline.

AI may be on your radar, but it's not part of how your business operates. Your team may be curious. You may have tested a few prompts. But there's no system, no organizational clarity, and no operating shift underway.

The risk isn't that you're behind today. The risk is that you stay casual while someone in your market starts redesigning their business around speed, responsiveness, and lower labor intensity.

Your next steps:

1. Pick one core workflow that repeats every week.

2. Document it from start to finish.

3. Identify where time is lost, where rework happens, and where judgment is actually needed.

4. Train leadership on the difference between AI tools, automation, and agents.

5. Run one meaningful pilot in the next 30 days.

Don't start with ten tools. Start with one workflow.

Level 2: AI-Curious (11–20)

You've begun using AI, but mostly as a helper.

Someone is using it to write, summarize, brainstorm, or clean things up. That creates familiarity. But it's still personal productivity, not operational redesign.

At this level, businesses often confuse activity with progress.

Your next steps:

1. Stop evaluating AI by novelty and start evaluating it by workflow impact.

2. Create a list of your ten most repetitive business processes.

3. Choose the top three based on volume, pain, and business value.

4. Establish simple rules for human review and approval.

5. Assign one person to own AI implementation instead of leaving it to random experimentation.

Your goal now is to move from curiosity to structure.

Level 3: Assisted Operations (21–30)

You're getting real value.

AI is helping across multiple parts of the business. Some automations may already be in place. The team is starting to trust the outputs. You're no longer asking whether AI matters.

This is the stage where many companies stall. Assisted operations feels productive enough. They get some time savings, some efficiency, some cleaner output—and stop before redesigning how work itself gets done.

Your next steps:

1. Break one recurring role into smaller decision blocks and task blocks.

2. Identify what can be drafted, monitored, routed, researched, or followed up automatically.

3. Design your first true specialist agent or agentic workflow.

4. Start measuring before-and-after performance.

5. Build a lightweight governance model with approval thresholds and escalation rules.

The question changes from "Can we use AI?" to "Which work should never require a human first touch again?"

Level 4: Workflow-Driven (31–40)

You're no longer experimenting randomly. You're designing.

Your workflows are clearer. Leadership sees AI as operational infrastructure. You understand that the opportunity isn't just faster content or fewer admin hours—it's better architecture.

This is where meaningful advantage starts to appear. You're building a business that responds faster, executes with more consistency, and compounds learning across systems.

Your next steps:

1. Define a formal hybrid org chart: humans, software, automations, and emerging agents.

2. Create named digital roles tied to clear outcomes.

3. Build memory and context handling more intentionally.

4. Establish KPI ownership for each major AI-enabled workflow.

5. Audit trust boundaries: what can run, what can draft, what must escalate.

Stop thinking in isolated automations. Start thinking in coordinated systems.

Level 5: Agent-Powered (41–50)

You're building the future on purpose.

Your business is actively architected around digital workers, structured workflows, escalation paths, and leadership oversight. AI isn't an accessory. It's becoming part of the operating system.

You're still early. Everyone is. But you're early in the right way.

The challenge now isn't adoption. It's discipline. Agent-powered businesses win when they stay grounded in governance, measurement, role clarity, and business reality. They lose when they drift into hype, complexity, or sloppy oversight.

Your next steps:

1. Keep tightening governance and auditability.

2. Expand only where there's measurable business impact.

3. Strengthen shared memory and context architecture.

4. Build resilience: exception handling, failure recovery, and human override paths.

5. Continue redesigning the company around compounding execution advantage.

This is where the gap widens between companies that use AI and companies structurally built for the next decade.

The Five Questions That Matter Most

If you remember nothing else from this diagnostic, remember these:

1. Where are we still dependent on human memory when we should be dependent on system design?

2. Which recurring workflows create the most friction, delay, or inconsistency?

3. What work truly requires human judgment, and what only requires disciplined execution?

4. Where could a specialist agent create speed without creating unacceptable risk?

5. Are we experimenting with AI, or are we redesigning the business around it?

That last question is the one that matters.

The companies that win this cycle won't be the ones that played with AI first. They'll be the ones that rebuilt around it first.

Take the interactive version of this diagnostic at **twiceahead.com/diagnostic** to receive your personalized score breakdown, customized recommendations for your level, and resources to help you take the next step.

Appendix B
Recommended Agent Stack for SMBs

Most small and mid-size businesses make the same mistake when they start exploring AI.

They ask, "Which tool should I buy?"

Wrong question.

The better question is, "Which business outcome am I trying to improve, and what kind of agent capability would help me do it?"

Tools matter. Models matter. Platforms matter. But if you start with vendors, you'll end up with a pile of subscriptions instead of a working system.

This appendix gives business owners a practical way to think about their first agent stack. It's organized by use case, not by vendor. That matters because the right stack for a title company, a law firm, a marketing agency, a contractor, or a healthcare group may include different products—but the underlying business functions are remarkably similar.

Think of this as a decision framework, not a shopping list.

Note: Because specific tools and models change rapidly, I maintain an up-to-date list of recommended platforms, models, and vendor options at **tw iceahead.com/stack**. Use this appendix to understand what you need. Use the website to find what's current.

A Simple Way to Think About the Stack

An effective SMB agent stack usually includes five layers:

1. Core models — the reasoning engines doing the thinking, drafting, analysis, and decision support.

2. Work interfaces — the chat, workspace, or front-end environment where humans interact with AI.

3. Workflow and automation layer — the system that moves information, triggers actions, and connects tools.

4. Business system layer — your CRM, help desk, email, calendar, file storage, and operating software.

5. Governance layer — permissions, approval rules, logging, escalation, and human oversight.

Most SMBs don't need the most advanced version of each layer on day one. They need a stack that solves real problems, can evolve, and is simple enough that the team will actually use it.

Start With Use Cases, Not Hype

A good first agent use case usually has four traits: it repeats frequently, it eats time, it follows recognizable patterns, and a mistake would be inconvenient but not catastrophic.

That's why the first wins usually show up in intake, routing, research, drafting, follow-up, content support, internal reporting, meeting prep, and task coordination.

That's also why you should not start by handing an unsupervised agent your finances, legal decisions, or high-risk compliance work.

1. The Executive Assistant Stack

This is one of the best starting points for most SMBs. The goal isn't to create a fake human assistant. It's to reduce mental clutter, improve responsiveness, and make sure important things don't get dropped.

Core functions: Email triage and draft responses. Meeting prep. Calendar coordination. Follow-up reminders. Daily briefing summaries. Task capture and prioritization. Basic research for calls and opportunities.

What matters most: Strong summarization. Reliable drafting. Good reasoning over written context. Calendar and email integration. Clear approval workflows before anything sensitive goes out.

Good first use case: A morning executive brief that pulls calendar items, open tasks, recent key emails, and meeting notes into one actionable summary. Immediate value, no reckless risk.

2. The Customer Intake and Routing Stack

A lot of SMBs lose money before the real work even starts. Leads sit. Requests get missed. Emails get forwarded manually. Forms go into black holes. Nobody knows who owns the next step.

This is exactly the kind of operational mess that agents can fix.

Core functions: Lead intake. Form processing. Inquiry categorization and qualification. Routing to the correct person or team. Auto-acknowledgment and follow-up. CRM updates.

What matters most: Classification and tagging. Structured data extraction from emails and forms. CRM integration. Rules-based routing. Human review when a request is ambiguous or high-value.

Good first use case: Every inbound inquiry is categorized automatically, entered into the CRM, assigned to an owner, and acknowledged within minutes. Not glamorous. Just good business.

3. The Sales Follow-Up Stack

Many SMBs don't have a lead problem. They have a follow-up problem. The opportunity isn't in replacing the salesperson. It's in making sure no prospect falls through the cracks and no conversation loses context.

Core functions: Follow-up reminders. Personalized outreach drafts. Call prep and objection summaries. Conversation recaps. Pipeline updates. Re-engagement sequences. Deal risk monitoring.

What matters most: Strong writing with context awareness. CRM integration. Access to past communication history. Clear boundaries around what can be auto-sent versus approved first.

Good first use case: After every sales call, the system generates a summary, updates the CRM, identifies next steps, and drafts a follow-up email for approval. That alone can transform consistency.

4. The Customer Service and Support Stack

Support is where operational friction becomes visible. Customers wait. The same questions get answered repeatedly. Internal teams waste time finding information that should be easy to access.

Core functions: FAQ handling. Ticket triage. Response drafting. Internal knowledge retrieval. Escalation to humans. After-hours response continuity.

What matters most: Access to approved knowledge sources. Fast classification. Escalation rules. Good retrieval over documents and help content. Guardrails to prevent confident nonsense.

Good first use case: Routine questions are answered instantly from approved company knowledge, while anything unusual, emotional, urgent, or high-risk gets routed to a human.

5. The Marketing and Content Stack

This is where many businesses start because the results are visible fast. That's fine, as long as they don't mistake content generation for full AI transformation. Marketing is a useful proving ground. It's just not the whole game.

Core functions: Content ideation. Drafting blogs, emails, ads, and social posts. Repurposing long-form content into shorter assets. Research support. Campaign planning. Basic performance summaries.

What matters most: Strong drafting and rewriting. Brand voice consistency. Workflow support for approvals and publishing. A central brand brief so output stays consistent.

Good first use case: One long-form founder video or webinar gets turned into email copy, LinkedIn posts, short-form social captions, blog outlines, and internal talking points. A real productivity win. Just don't stop there.

6. The Operations and Back-Office Stack

This is where real leverage starts showing up. Back-office work is full of repetitive motion: internal handoffs, checklist monitoring, status updates, reporting, document routing, exception handling, and compliance-adjacent review. Fertile ground for agentic workflows.

Core functions: Checklist monitoring. Internal status updates. Data reconciliation support. Document handling. Exception spotting. Task creation and routing. Reporting and dashboard narratives.

What matters most: Structured reasoning. Rules plus AI working together. Clear escalation paths. Strong integration with business systems. Auditability.

Good first use case: An operations monitor checks open work every day, flags exceptions, drafts status summaries, and routes next actions to the correct owner. The beginning of a digital operations layer.

7. The Knowledge and Training Stack

Many SMBs do a poor job of preserving what the business knows. That becomes painful when people leave, when new hires ramp slowly, or when the founder remains the bottleneck because the real answers live in their head.

Core functions: Internal knowledge retrieval. SOP creation and cleanup. Onboarding support. Training materials. Policy guidance. Role-specific playbooks.

What matters most: Good retrieval from internal documentation. Strong summarization. Easy searchability. Version control and content governance. Role-specific outputs.

Good first use case: New hires can ask how a process works, retrieve the approved SOP, and get a role-specific summary without waiting for the founder or manager. That's not just efficiency. That's organizational maturity.

8. The Specialty Agent Stack

After the basics are working, many SMBs can justify specialist digital roles. These aren't generic assistants. They're purpose-built agents tied to a defined business function.

Examples: a recruiting support agent, a contract review pre-check agent, a finance variance monitor, a compliance prep agent, a transaction coordinator support agent, a project manager agent, a franchise support agent, a municipal research agent.

The test for specialization: Is the use case frequent enough to justify it? Are the inputs and outputs clear enough to standardize? Can the agent operate inside acceptable trust boundaries? Is there a human owner for escalation and review?

Good first use case: A specialist agent that prepares work for humans instead of pretending to replace them. That's almost always the smarter starting position.

Model Strategy for SMBs

Business owners don't need to become model experts, but they need a practical framework. Most SMBs should evaluate models in four categories:

General reasoning and drafting models. Your workhorse. Writing, summarization, planning, analysis, and business support.

Fast, lower-cost utility models. Lighter tasks: triage, tagging, classification, and high-volume operations where cost matters.

Multimodal models. Work across text, images, documents, screenshots, charts, and other visual material.

Specialized models or services. Transcription, image generation, coding, voice, or other narrower functions.

The right move for most SMBs isn't to bet everything on one model forever. It's to build a stack that can evolve as models improve.

For current model recommendations and comparisons, visit **twiceahead.co m/stack**.

Platform Strategy for SMBs

When evaluating platforms, focus on these questions: Can it connect to the systems we already use? Can it support approval workflows? Can it preserve context or memory where needed? Can we see what happened if something goes wrong? Can a non-technical operator manage it after setup? Will the team actually adopt it?

That last question matters more than people think. The best stack on paper is worthless if it's too fragile, too complex, or too annoying for daily use.

A Practical Starter Stack for Most SMBs

If I were advising a typical small or mid-size business to begin, I'd usually recommend something like this:

Layer 1: One premium general-purpose AI workspace. Used by leadership and key operators for drafting, analysis, summarization, and work support.

Layer 2: One workflow automation platform. Used to connect forms, CRM, email, calendars, tickets, spreadsheets, and business apps.

Layer 3: Your existing core business systems. CRM, help desk, project management, file storage, email, and line-of-business software.

Layer 4: One internal knowledge source. A clean, approved repository of SOPs, FAQs, process notes, and business context.

Layer 5: Governance rules. Defined approval thresholds, human review checkpoints, and clear decisions about what can be automated versus what must escalate.

That's enough to get serious traction. You don't need a science project. You need a working operating layer.

What to Avoid Early

Buying too many tools too early. A bloated stack creates confusion, cost, and poor adoption.

Starting with the most technical use cases. High-risk compliance or mission-critical decision-making increases the odds of failure.

Treating prompts as a strategy. A good prompt can help. It's not an operating model.

Ignoring workflow design. Bad processes don't become good processes because AI touches them.

No owner, no accountability. If nobody owns the AI rollout, random experimentation will masquerade as progress.

The Right Way to Build the Stack

Here's the sequence I recommend:

1. Pick one workflow that matters.

2. Define the outcome.

3. Identify the systems involved.

4. Decide where AI can assist, where automation should route, and where a human must approve.

5. Launch a narrow pilot.

6. Measure speed, quality, responsiveness, and error reduction.

7. Only then expand.

That's how real agent capability gets built. Not through hype. Not through tool collecting. Through disciplined workflow design tied to business value.

Final Thought

The best SMB agent stack isn't the most expensive one, the most technical one, or the one with the most logos on the slide.

It's the one that helps your business think faster, respond faster, and operate with more consistency—without creating chaos.

Build for usefulness first. Trust second. Scale third.

Do that well, and your first agent stack becomes the beginning of a very different kind of company.

For recommended tools, current model comparisons, and platform guides, visit **twiceahead.com/stack**.

Appendix C
Plain-English Glossary of Agentic AI Terms

Most business leaders don't need more jargon. They need clear language.

A lot of confusion around AI comes from people using the same words to mean different things. One person says "agent" and means a chatbot. Another means a fully autonomous system. One vendor says "memory" and means temporary chat history. Another means a persistent operating layer that carries context forward over time.

This glossary is designed to fix that. The definitions below are written for operators, founders, and executives. They're practical on purpose.

Agent

An AI system designed to perform work toward a goal, not just answer a question.

A basic chatbot waits for you to ask something. An agent can be given a role, an objective, access to tools, and boundaries for how it should operate. It may gather information, make recommendations, draft outputs, trigger actions, or hand work off when it reaches a limit.

Think of an agent less like a search engine and more like a junior digital worker with defined responsibilities.

Agent Stack

The collection of models, interfaces, workflow tools, integrations, business systems, and governance layers used to build AI capabilities inside the company. Not one tool—the operating setup behind the work.

Agentic AI

AI organized to take action, pursue goals, and participate in workflows—instead of simply generating one-off answers.

It doesn't mean magic. It means the AI is being used inside a structure that gives it direction, context, and a job to do.

Agentic Workflow

A business process where AI does more than assist with one step. Instead of just writing a draft, the system may review inputs, classify information, prepare the next action, route work, escalate exceptions, and keep the process moving.

A workflow with some degree of AI-driven execution built into it.

API

A structured way for one software system to communicate with another. Business leaders don't need to become technical experts here. The practical point is that APIs are what make workflows and agents able to interact with the rest of the business.

Approval Threshold

The point at which human signoff is required. This may be based on dollar amount, customer importance, legal risk, confidence score, or type of action. Not every action needs approval. Important actions usually do.

Audit Trail

The record of what happened, when it happened, who or what did it, and what information was used. Matters for accountability, troubleshooting, compliance, and trust.

Augmentation

AI helps a human perform better, faster, or more consistently. The human is still driving the work, but AI improves the output. This is where most businesses start.

Autonomous

A system that can perform work with limited human intervention. There are degrees of autonomy. The more steps a system can complete correctly without waiting for a human, the more autonomous it is.

Autonomy Threshold

The point at which you're willing to let the system act without prior approval.

You may allow an agent to summarize emails automatically, but not to send a response without review. That boundary is an autonomy threshold. Every smart business sets these deliberately.

Confidence Threshold

The minimum level of certainty required before the system can proceed automatically. If confidence falls below that line, the work gets flagged for review or escalated.

Context

The background information the AI needs to do useful work: the task, the goal, the customer history, the company rules, prior conversation, role instructions, or relevant business data. Poor context usually leads to weak outputs.

Context Window

The amount of information a model can consider at one time. If too much is stuffed in, important details may get lost or dropped.

For business leaders, the takeaway is simple: more context isn't always better. Better-structured context is better.

Copilot

An AI assistant that works alongside a human user, helping with drafting, summarization, research, or suggestions. It usually doesn't act independently unless told to.

A copilot supports the person. An agent increasingly supports the process.

Digital Worker

A practical business term for an AI-driven role that performs recurring work inside the company. It may not be fully autonomous and may still require oversight, but it behaves more like an operating role than a one-time software feature.

Drift

The gradual loss of consistency over time. An agent that once performed well may begin producing weaker results because context changed, instructions became messy, data quality slipped, or the workflow was altered carelessly. One reason AI systems need active management.

Escalation

Handing work from the AI system to a human when the matter is too risky, too ambiguous, too emotional, too important, or outside defined boundaries. A strong AI system knows when not to pretend.

Exception Handling

What happens when the process encounters something unusual: missing information, a conflicting instruction, an angry customer, a system outage, a policy violation, or a case that doesn't fit the normal pattern.

A mature business designs for exceptions instead of pretending they won't happen.

Failure Recovery

The process for restoring safe operation when something breaks: rolling back a change, disabling a workflow, rerouting to a human, or restoring a prior configuration. Smart businesses plan for recovery before they need it.

Fine-Tuning

A method of adapting a model more specifically to certain behaviors or types of output. Most SMBs don't need to start here. Good context, strong instructions, and better workflow design usually matter more.

First Human Touch

The point where a person first becomes involved in a process. In many traditional businesses, a human touches almost everything first. In an agent-powered business, the goal is often to push human involvement later—into judgment, exception handling, and relationship-critical moments.

Generalist Agent

An agent that handles a wider variety of tasks but usually with less focus than a specialist. Generalists can be useful early on, especially for founders and small teams, but over time many businesses benefit from creating more role-specific agents.

Governance

The broader management system around AI use. It includes policy, accountability, approvals, review standards, risk boundaries, auditability, and ownership. Guardrails are part of governance. Governance is the full discipline.

Grounding

Anchoring the AI's answer or action in reliable source material. A grounded system is less likely to invent information because it's working from approved data, documents, or system records.

Guardrails

The rules and limits placed around what an AI system can do: access controls, approval requirements, prohibited actions, escalation rules, tone rules, policy instructions, or confidence thresholds.

How you keep AI useful without letting it become reckless.

Hallucination

When an AI confidently states something that is false, unsupported, or made up. This is one of the biggest reasons governance matters.

In a business setting, a hallucination can create customer confusion, bad decisions, reputational damage, or compliance risk.

Human in the Loop

A human reviews, approves, or participates before the process moves forward. For example, an agent may draft a client email, but a human approves it before it's sent. One of the most practical models for early-stage AI deployment.

Human on the Loop

The system operates more independently, while a human monitors outcomes, exceptions, or performance from above. The human isn't involved in every step but remains accountable for oversight.

Hybrid Workforce

A company structure that includes humans, software systems, automations, and AI agents working together. This is the direction I believe most serious businesses are heading. The future isn't purely human and it isn't purely autonomous. It's coordinated.

Integration

A connection between systems so information can move between them. If the CRM, help desk, email, calendar, and document repository don't connect well, the AI layer will usually underperform.

Knowledge Base

The organized body of documents, FAQs, procedures, policies, and reference material the business wants people and systems to use. If your knowledge base is sloppy, your AI outputs will often be sloppy too.

KPI

Key performance indicator. When applied to AI: the metric you care about—time saved, speed to response, conversion lift, error reduction, cycle time improvement, customer satisfaction, or margin improvement. If there's no KPI, it's easy to confuse excitement with impact.

Memory

How an AI system retains useful information over time. Some memory is short-lived, like a current chat. Some is persistent, meaning important facts, instructions, or project history can be reused across future work.

Memory matters because repeated work gets better when the system doesn't start from zero every time.

Memory Architecture

The design of how context is stored, organized, retrieved, and reused. That includes what gets remembered, where it lives, how long it persists, who can access it, and when it should be updated.

Good memory architecture improves consistency. Bad memory architecture creates confusion, drift, and errors.

Model

The underlying AI engine that does the reasoning, writing, analysis, or interpretation. Different models have different strengths, speeds, and costs. The important question isn't which model is coolest—it's which model is best suited for the task.

Multi-Agent System

A setup where more than one agent works together. One agent may research. Another may draft. Another may review for policy or quality. Another may route the result to a human.

Complex business work often requires specialization, not one giant all-purpose AI blob.

Multimodal

The system can work with more than one kind of input: text, images, documents, screenshots, charts, or audio. Increasingly important as business work goes beyond plain text.

Orchestrator

The coordinating layer that decides which step happens next, which tool or agent gets used, and when work should escalate to a human.

If you imagine a team of specialists, the orchestrator is the manager making sure the right task goes to the right role at the right time.

Pilot

A controlled test of a new AI capability in a narrow environment. Good pilots are specific: an owner, a time frame, a success definition, and a clear decision about what happens next.

Production

The system is being used in real operations, not just tested in experiments. A production system affects actual work, real customers, real staff, and real outcomes. That's where discipline becomes non-negotiable.

Prompt

The instruction you give an AI system. That can be as simple as a question or as complex as a structured operating instruction.

Prompts matter, but a business should never confuse prompting skill with systems design. A great prompt is not a substitute for a great workflow.

Retrieval

Pulling in the right information from documents, systems, or knowledge sources at the moment it's needed. This helps the AI work from approved material instead of guessing.

ROI

Return on investment. In this context, it answers a simple question: is the AI system creating enough business value to justify the time, money, complexity, and oversight required to run it?

Role Design

The process of defining who or what is responsible for a business outcome. In an agent-powered business, role design applies to both humans and digital workers. Clear responsibilities matter because if everything is vague, nothing scales well.

Specialist Agent

An agent designed for one narrow role or type of work. Examples: intake triage, support ticket classification, meeting prep, report generation, or follow-up drafting.

Specialists are often more reliable than trying to make one agent do everything.

Structured Data

Information stored in a consistent, organized format: fields in a CRM, spreadsheet columns, database records, form entries, or tagged ticket data. Structured data is easier for systems to process reliably than messy notes buried in email threads.

Tool Use

When an AI system can call on other software or services to perform actions or gather information—searching the web, reading files, updating a CRM, checking a calendar, sending a message, or generating a report. An agent becomes much more useful when it can do more than generate text.

Unstructured Data

Information that doesn't live in clean fields. Emails, PDFs, call transcripts, chat history, documents, voice notes, and freeform text all fall into this category. A lot of business value is trapped here.

Workflow Automation

Using software rules, triggers, and integrations to move work automatically from one step to another. This may or may not involve AI. Automation moves tasks. Agentic systems help make decisions within that movement.

Final Thought

You don't need to memorize every term in this glossary.

What matters is understanding the shift behind the language. The old world was software as a tool. The new world is software, workflows, and agents operating together inside the business.

Once you see that clearly, the jargon starts mattering less—and the business design starts mattering a lot more.

About the Author

Thomas Heimann is an AI-native business builder, entrepreneur, and operator who helps founders redesign their companies around agentic workflows, digital workers, and autonomous operating systems.

Long before AI, he was an internet pioneer. He coined the term *autoresponder* in 1994, built the first web-based domain registration service in 1995, and founded GEN—which grew into the world's largest web hosting provider, serving more than 35,000 domains for 10,000 customers across 30+ countries. He co-created the eBusiness CD-ROM with Microsoft and AOL to accelerate small-business adoption of ecommerce.

Today he is the founder and CEO of Cloud Title, where he's building an AI-native title and settlement company, and is actively deploying multi-agent AI systems on OpenClaw to power operations across his businesses. He lives in Tampa Bay, Florida, with his wife Jennifer.